ISLE OF WIGHT THEN & NOW

IN COLOUR

JAN TOMS

To my family and friends – you know who you are!

First published in 2012, this edition 2014

The History Press
The Mill, Brimscombe Port
Stroud, Gloucestershire, GL5 2QG
www.thehistorypress.co.uk

British Library Cataloguing in Publication Data.
A catalogue record for this book is available from the British Library.

ISBN 978 0 7509 6206 3

Typesetting and origination by The History Press
Printed in India.

CONTENTS

ACKNOWLEDGEMENTS

While every care has been taken to ensure that the pictures included in this book do not infringe copyright, should anyone feel that their right of ownership has been infringed, the author apologises and requests that they get in touch through the publisher.

Particular thanks go to the following people who freely supplied photographs: Carisbrooke Castle Museum Gallery (carismus@lineone.net), for seven pictures; Mr Terence Westmore, for the picture of the Chad Rock, Blackgang; Julia Margaret Cameron Trust, for two images of Dimbola Lodge, Freshwater Bay; Robin McInnes, for the picture of Tower Cottage, Shanklin and the Old Park, St Lawrence; Ray Doe, for the picture of The Mount and Yarmouth Harbour; Teresa Day, for the picture of Appley Towers, Ryde; Alan Stroud, for the picture of Church Litten, Newport; Brian Greening, for the picture of The Malt House, and Newport Electricity Station; S. and H. Lloyd, for the picture of The White House, Parkhurst; Rob Jennings, for the picture of The Spithead Hotel, Bembridge; Mr Caws, for the picture of Thorley Chapel; The Barber Shop, Freshwater, for the picture of Moa Place; Bob West, for the picture of Isaac Sheath's house at Chale; Kevin Mitchell, for the picture of The Five Bells Inn, Brighstone; W.J. Nigh of Shanklin, for the postcard of Lake High Street; The Isle of Wight Steam Railway, Havenstreet, for the picture of Sandown Railway Station.

Thank you also to the Public Record Office Newport (record.office@iow.gov.uk) for permission to use twelve pictures from their archive.

I am particularly grateful to Mr Brian Manser at Parkhurst Prison; Mrs Chris Yendell, curator at Carisbrooke Castle Museum; Mr Michael Hunter at Osborne House; the staff of Newport Public Record Office; plus all those who generously gave information.

INTRODUCTION

In the 1850s, the Isle of Wight experienced a revolution. Remote shoreline hamlets found themselves taken over by Victorian pleasure-seekers, who proceeded to replace the tumbledown stone cottages with smart brick villas. The catalyst was the arrival of the steam railway.

A century earlier, other enterprising gentlemen had already discovered the benefits of a balmy climate, establishing imposing bolt-holes away from the hub-bub of mainland life. Here they built prestigious mansions with towers, turrets and landscaped gardens, providing new job opportunities for native Islanders.

By the late twentieth century, the process was already being reversed as those mighty castles, halls and mansions, inconvenient and expensive to maintain, fell to the march of progress. Commandeered by the wartime army, misused then neglected, their demise was guaranteed. In their place has sprung up acres of bungalow estates. The railway, meanwhile, has all but vanished.

The process of change continues.

Jan Toms, 2012

THE CHAD ROCK, BLACKGANG

THE OLD COAST road from Niton to Blackgang passed through spectacular scenery. On the landward side, the near vertical layered strata of Gore Cliff loomed above, while below, the sea provided a show of ever-changing moods and colours. Head straight out into the water and the next landmass would be South America.

Along this road, at Windy Corner, stood the Chad Rock, a boulder towering over 40ft in height, dwarfing coaches and causing passengers to raise their eyes heavenwards. It may have stood on this spot for anything up to 10,000 years when the coastline was laid down at the end of the Ice Age.

Because of the peculiar pairing of upper greensand stone, layered with gault clay known locally as blue slipper, the entire area along the Undercliff was in constant danger of landslide. In 1799, locals saw what they thought was an optical illusion as nearby Pitlands Farm appeared to be moving slowly towards the sea. Along with a hundred acres of land it indeed slid seawards, the farm disappearing into a chasm. Two people lost their lives. Over the next hundred years, other landslides occurred, then, in 1928, a fall of monumental

proportions closed the Blackgang to Niton road forever. Over night, 140,000 tons of rock fell, taking part of the road with it. When the dust settled, the Chad Rock was still there, stubbornly claiming its traditional place in the tumbling landscape.

HOW THE CHAD ROCK got its name is not recorded. St Chad, the seventh-century Anglo-Saxon bishop, seems to have been associated mainly with northern England. Chad is not a local name. The boulder also became known as the Salisbury Rock because, on its flat surface, the image of Lord Salisbury was said to be visible.

When the Second World War broke out, Island beaches were barricaded off and gun emplacements replaced tourists. After the war, locals returned to this once familiar spot and the first thing they noticed was the absence of the Chad Rock. The Island had taken its share of aerial bombardment and it was thought that the iconic landmark had received a direct hit from an enemy bomb. The truth was infinitely sadder. In order to test its explosive power the army had targeted the rock, eventually blowing it out of existence. Thus, a piece of Island landscape disappeared forever. Today, no sign of the rock or the coach road remains.

DIMBOLA LODGE, FRESHWATER BAY

AN EARLY ENGRAVING of Freshwater Bay shows two cottages standing on the incline above the sea. These were the property of Jacob Long a local fisherman who, in 1860, took advantage of a sudden interest in the area to sell them to a wealthy couple named Cameron. The Camerons must have seemed an exotic pair. Charles Hay was a legal expert retired from the Indian service while his younger wife, Julia Margaret, was the daughter of a French lady aristocrat.

The Camerons were delighted both by the magic of the Bay and the opportunity to live almost next door to the Tennysons at Farringford. Julia immediately had the cottages renovated and joined together by means of a central tower, but then Charles was called away to sort out difficulties in his plantations in Ceylon. Left behind, Julia found an increasingly absorbing hobby in photography.

In South Africa she had met the chemist and astronomer Sir John Herschal, who planted an interest in the new technology. In London, her sister, Sarah Princep, introduced her to a circle of artists and literati. Soon, waves of these illustrious visitors were invited to her Freshwater house, Dimbola Lodge, named for the Camerons' estate in Ceylon. Undeterred by the lengthy and often toxic business of coating glass plates and developing negatives, Julia threw herself into photographing visitors and locals alike. Inspired by the fashion for creating *tableaux vivants*, she commandeered children and workmen to pose for scenes from classical and biblical stories. Happily organising her neighbour, Lord Tennyson, she undertook to produce illustrations for his numerous works, in particular the Arthurian *Idylls of the King*.

Julia and Charles returned to Ceylon in 1875. During her Island stay Julia had photographed, among others, Charles Darwin, Lewis Carol, H.W. Longfellow, G.D. Rossetti, G.F. Watts, Charles Kingsley and Robert Browning. In total she produced about 200 images.

BY 1900, ARTHUR Ralph Douglas Elliot, Liberal MP and Secretary to the Treasury, was living at Dimbola. Later it was divided into two, one half, known as Cameron House, becoming a lodging house. Gradually its condition declined. Viewed increasingly as an eyesore, the council approved plans to pull it down and erect a block of flats.

A group of dismayed locals campaigned to get the planning permission overturned and almost within hours of the house's demolition it was saved. The long, dedicated commitment of enthusiasts has transformed it into a photographic museum.

The year 1970 saw the last public recorded performance of guitar legend Jimi Hendrix on nearby Afton Down. In memory of the then biggest ever pop festival, a life-size statue of Hendrix by sculptor John Swindells stands in Dimbola's garden.

TOWER COTTAGE, SHANKLIN

DURING THE EARLY nineteenth century, the rustic idyll of peasant houses began to appeal to the wealthy and it became fashionable to build a 'cottage orne'; a large, comfortable house with all mod-cons while aping the rural simplicity of country dwellings.

The first to be built in Shanklin was Tower Cottage, on the edge of Shanklin Chine and surrounded by a two-acre garden. It was erected in 1825 for General Sir James Viney, who leased the land from the White Popham Estate. Traditionally, such leases were for three lives, so the General named himself, his son and – surely a piece of social climbing – Princess Victoria, the future Queen of England.

The General fought under Wellington in the Peninsular War, commanding the artillery at the Battle of Corunna. On his return home, however, things were not as peaceful as he might have hoped.

By 1827 he was in financial difficulties and rapidly began mortgaging his various properties. His mental health deteriorated and he died in 1841.

It was his niece, Lady Beconsfield, wife of future Prime Minister Benjamin d'Israeli, who became his heiress. Neither she nor the next named lessee – by this time Queen Victoria, ever took up residence.

This pretty, seven-bedroom, thatched cottage had a double drawing room, a dining room and a round, ivy-covered tower. French casement doors opened onto the veranda and there was carriage access from Chine Avenue. A secret tunnel starting at the fisherman's cottage at the bottom of the Chine supposedly led right up to Tower Cottage for the purpose of bringing contraband ashore. At some point the tunnel was blocked by a fall so that access was lost.

FOR MORE THAN fifty years, Campbell Cameron Esq. occupied the house until the death of Miss Jane Cameron, in 1908. Thereafter it passed through several hands. In 1915, Jane Elizabeth Collis, a widow, took the cottage for the summer and by 1929 Mr Arthur Lewenstein, a Polish inventor, lived there. In September 1932 the house was put up for auction. By this time the interior had been modernised with the provision of gas, electricity, central heating and a telephone room.

By the 1940s, however, a combination of natural slippage and a good shaking when a bomb landed nearby, forced the occupants to leave amid rumours that they were German spies signalling to enemy shipping from the tower.

Left standing empty, within three years half the cottage fell away. The council took possession, converting the kitchens into public toilets. By 1951 it was declared so dangerous that it was finally demolished.

THE MOUNT, YARMOUTH

LEAVING YARMOUTH, THE Newport road rises quickly to a plateau. Here once stood The Mount, the largest house ever to be built in the town.

It was erected by the Revd George Burrard, a wealthy clergyman. In 1801, he was appointed chaplain to King George III and presented to the living of Yarmouth by the Lord Chancellor. Purchasing some land, by 1809 the Mount was ready for occupation. The site could not have been better. To the north was an uninterrupted view of the Solent while to the south the vista of Yarmouth marsh provided a watery expanse colonised by migrant birds.

The Revd George was variously MP for Lymington, MP for Yarmouth and Commissioner of Customs for the Port of London. When he died his second wife, Edith, remained at The Mount. Her grandchildren, Roland and Edith Cooper, came to live with her and on 15 August 1866 young Edith married the Revd Robert Lewis Dashwood from nearby Westhill House. The wedding was a huge occasion. The bride had fourteen attendants while 220 schoolchildren were treated to tea and cake. As the young couple left for a Continental honeymoon, the event was rounded off with fireworks.

Dashwood was a Church of England minister. In 1905, he recorded all the oil paintings, watercolours, pastels, miniatures and photographs displayed in the house, totalling 385. The paintings included works by George Stubbs, George Romney, Sir Peter Lely and George Morland.

Robert and Edith produced seven children, of whom four did not marry. Denying any relationship to Sir Francis Dashwood, founder of the scandalous

Hellfire Club, Theresa, Cuthbert, Constance and Caroline lived at The Mount, leading lives of Christian goodness. The poor of the parish relied on their help and the Dashwood sisters supplied layettes for needy babies, coal for the poor, and augmented the organist's salary. The RSPCA and the Girls' Friendly Society also benefited.

AS THE DASHWOODS grew old, their savings dwindled. Rooms in The Mount stood empty as they retreated to their childhood domain in the nursery. Carriages mouldered in the cobbled yard, the servants' quarters fell silent and the house no longer echoed to musical evenings or laughter from the croquet lawn. The last Miss Dashwood, Constance, died at the age of 89 in 1966, still looked after by a gardener and housekeeper.

In Yarmouth there was a scheme to re-align the main road. The house's foundations were declared suspect and the only possible route for the highway was through the old Georgian building. So, The Mount was condemned and the A3053 now runs over its ghost while an estate of modern houses fills its gardens. A road name alone bears witness to its existence.

THE OLD PARK, ST LAWRENCE

IN 1881, GERMAN chemist William Spindler bought a retirement home at St Lawrence. He went to great trouble to find it, having dismissed Bournemouth, Torquay, Brighton, Weymouth and the Channel Islands in its favour. In the same year he became a naturalised Englishman. Spindler may have retired but he came with ambitious plans to create his own seaside resort intended to rival Ventnor.

The Old Park had been part of the 2,300-acre Appuldurcombe estate and in 1782 it was in the hands of Charles Anderson Pelham, who found Appuldurcombe, an excellent base from which to pursue his sailing activities. He leased off the land at Old Park to a Mr John Harvey and, on Harvey's death in 1820, it was sold to a London solicitor named Thomas Haddon.

Haddon began a major makeover, creating a cottage orne with a landscaped garden, lake, a bathing house and walled vineyard. However, too much extravagance – blamed on his wife –

meant that he went bankrupt and the house and its contents were put up for sale. The Old Park then passed through the hands of Captain Bowles, Captain Beard and Josiah Horton before being purchased by Sir John Cheape, a soldier for the East India Company and *aide-de-campe* to Queen Victoria. Cheape constructed the east wing of the house and filled in Haddon's lake. He died at the Old Park on 30 March 1875 and his daughter sold it to William Spindler.

Spindler began constructing a sea wall intended to extend from Binnel Bay to Ventnor. The sea, however, had other ideas, literally dashing his ambitions. Undaunted, he donated Ventnor Park to the local people and saw the construction of Park Road and the Whitwell Road. In Whitwell itself, where he was a regular member of the congregation, he paid for the installation of a water supply, a peal of bells and a clock for the church.

It was at the Old Park, however, where he was busiest. In seven years he installed central heating, double-glazing, a huge underground reservoir for water, a kitchen garden and orchid house, and imported a million trees and shrubs to landscape the grounds. William died in 1889, his wife Clara remaining until her death in 1906.

WITH SPINDLER'S DEATH, his son and daughter quarrelled and simply left the estate in the hands of solicitors, where it remained. In 1948, a Mr Thornton, exploring the area, stumbled across the house buried in undergrowth. Discovering that it had been empty since 1906 he rescued it, adding another wing and running it as a hotel, a tropical bird park and a glass-blowing centre. The bird park is no longer there but the hotel and glass-blowing business remains.

APPLEY TOWERS, RYDE

TRAVEL ALONG RYDE SEAFRONT and you eventually come to the Appley Tower, a quaint folly at the water's edge. Once, a fine mock Tudor mansion stood on the rise above it. The house was built about 1840 for Mr George Young, a Scottish corn merchant. Employing local architect Thomas Hellyer, the design included a central tower and a clock tower over the east wing. With no great stretch of the imagination, Young named it Appley Towers. This new house included a park, gardens, farm, stables, a boathouse and three lodges. The Young family remained for nearly forty years.

There had already been several houses in the neighbourhood incorporating the name Appley and at some point the Hutt family seems to have acquired all of them. It was not surprising, therefore, that when Appley Towers became vacant, Sir William Hutt, formerly of Sturbridge House in Ryde, took possession.

William spent his career in the colonies. In New Zealand he acquired 20 million acres of Maori land by bartering weapons and trinkets. His name survives in both the Hutt River in Australia and Upper and Lower Hutt in Wellington, New Zealand. He died at Appley Towers in 1882.

The house then passed to his brother, George, a British Indian Army Officer. Like William, George had been born on the Island, rising to the rank of Major General, having a long career in the Indian subcontinent. He died at Appley Towers in 1889.

In 1907 tragedy struck when a fire came close to destroying the house. It then came into the ownership of Major General George's eldest son, George William Hutt. Like his father and uncle, he too died on the Island, aged just 46.

THE PROPERTY WAS then purchased by 43-year-old Sir Hedworth Williamson, the 9th baronet Williamson of Whitburn Hall in Durham. A mystery surrounded his mother, Lady Elizabeth Liddell, cousin of the Alice of *Alice in Wonderland* fame, for she disappeared without trace when out riding near Marsden Rock in South Shields. Sir Hedworth senior never recovered from his loss, giving away much of his wealth to family servants. His son, Sir Hedworth, lived at Appley Towers until his death in 1942.

By now the elegant old house had lost its appeal and during the 1960s it was pulled down to make way for redevelopment, however, several edifices survive. Along Appley Lane remain both Upper and Middle Lodge, quaint houses built for the gardeners, while at the bottom of the lane the old boathouse, quirky in its design, is utilised by Ryde Rowing Club.

Meanwhile, Appley Tower, that Victorian gothic folly constructed at the water's edge, was allegedly erected for the amusement of Mary of Teck, who married King George V. Finding Osborne tiresome, she often escaped to Appley Tower, while George amused himself on the water.

Happily, the public space of Appley Park is now in the hands of the Council and is open for everyone's pleasure.

POUND GREEN, FRESHWATER

UNSPOILT COUNTRY HAMLETS are hard to find. Coming upon Pound Green at Freshwater therefore is a gift. In its entirety, Freshwater was once made up of a series of small rural communities such as Easton, Weston, Norton, Middleton, Sheepwash, Stroud, School Green and Freshwater Bay.

Pound Green housed the village pound, where stray animals were enclosed until a fine was paid for their release. A pound would have been familiar to the Saxons and is still reflected in the word 'impounded'. The Pound itself is a small, circular, stone-built enclosure. English Heritage lists two on the Island, the other being at Brading.

Today, Pound Green consists of fourteen dwellings. Two, Lea Cottage and Little Halt, date back to at least the seventeenth century. Inevitably there was some building in Victorian times when small, brick-built villas were added, but the feel of the place remains unchanged.

In the mid-nineteenth century, one family dominated the hamlet – the Hilliers, providing labour for the surrounding farms. In 1851, John, Martha and their five children lived in Lea cottage. Living with them was John's 70-year-old mother, while next door was widow Hannah Oates, aged 75. The two older women were described as paupers. Their neighbours were Henry and Jane Hillier, with four daughters. Like John, Henry was described as a farm labourer. Nearby were also James and Jane Hillier. To make ends meet they took in a lodger, William Moyce, a baker. Along with the other residents, the Merwoods and the Osbourne Whites, without exception they had been born on the Island.

MARY ANN HILLIER, DAUGHTER of John and Martha, had an unforeseen claim to fame. At the age of fourteen she went to work as a parlour maid at Dimbola Lodge. Mary soon came to the notice of her employer Julia Margaret Cameron, who had developed an absorbing hobby in photography. Soon Mary's duties included posing for Mrs Cameron's dramatic tableaux. On several occasions she represented her namesake, the Virgin Mary. By the 1880s Mary had moved out of Pound Green, although not out of Freshwater, having married Thomas Gilbert, a gardener, and together they had eight children.

Only one new house has appeared in the last fifty years and that replaced an existing cottage in a market garden. The houses are a mix of stone and brick, some rendered, some painted white, and the roofs range from thatch to slate to tiles. Pound Green continues to exude an atmosphere of peace and tranquility.

THE THEATRE ROYAL, RYDE

IN JANUARY 1894, residents of Ryde turned out to watch a spectacular event at the Theatre Royal. The Hermann troupe of freed slaves was to put on a performance of *Uncle Tom's Cabin*. Thirty of the cast had indeed been slaves and entranced the audience by singing Negro spirituals. As if this were not novel enough, the audience also marvelled at a performance by Mr Alfred Loding and his boxing donkey! The Theatre Royal stood at the point where Upper and Lower Ryde meet, joined together by the appropriately named Union Street. To the theatre's right was the Crown Hotel and further down the hill the elegant spire of St Thomas's Church was visible through the trees. A lamp and drinking trough stood opposite for the convenience of man and horse. For nearly 200 years the Theatre Royal provided lavish entertainment.

MRS DOROTHY JORDAN, famous for dressing in male attire, made one of her last performances at the Theatre Royal in 1810. She was also famous for being the mistress of the future King William IV, having borne him ten children. Once William realised that he might inherit the throne he promptly cast Dorothy aside and looked for a suitable bride. His choice fell on the future Queen Adelaide, who failed to give him an heir. Dorothy retired to the Continent.

In the 1870s the Theatre Royal was enlarged and could accommodate 1,000 people. In the foyer the exotic atmosphere of a Palm Court greeted patrons, while famous performers included Sir Henry Irving and Ellen Terry. With the advent of the cinema films were also shown, gradually becoming the main source of entertainment.

How long the old theatre might have lasted we can only guess, but in May 1961 fire swept through it. The Theatre Royal had given its last performance. Past saving, it was demolished and from its ashes rose the NatWest Bank. The horse trough and lamp have long gone and St Thomas's Church stands empty and without its spire.

SHANKLIN LITERARY INSTITUTE

THE VICTORIAN ERA was great on civic pride and when it came to erecting public buildings, Shanklin was there with the best of them.

The year 1879 saw the opening of the new Institute at the top of Prospect Road. It was intended to provide a public meeting place and a venue for education. Built in classical style, above the three bays of the entrance the word INSTITUTE was emblazoned. By 1884, more money was raised to extend the building southwards to accommodate a Reading Room where, for the price of a penny, residents could avail themselves of the new facility. At the same time an Amusement Room offered entertainment in the form of billiards and chess. Shanklin Council changed the name from the wordy Shanklin Literary Institute and Reading Room, to the Town Hall.

In 1925 disaster struck, when a fire badly damaged the building. As a result a sum of £17,000 was voted for restoration work. By this time, however, Shanklin

Council had been amalgamated with Sandown and, in the way of such things, the councillors at Sandown were not happy to see such a huge amount spent on the rival resort. Finally, in 1932, with a reduced budget of £13,000, the go-ahead was given to refurbish the building. The finished result was a storey higher and extended outward to allow for an imposing foyer. While the outside remained classical in appearance, inside, Art Deco features appeared. It also gained another new name – Shanklin Town Hall and Theatre. The new theatre had a balcony and orchestra pit, and could accommodate an audience of 700. Seats in the auditorium were movable and audiences transformed into dancers beneath a huge glittering ball throwing rainbows across the room.

NOW BEGAN AN era of entertainment. Plays, concerts and variety shows filled the theatre, but the good times were disrupted by the Second World War. Behind closed doors the Town Hall became a nerve centre for operations while the Reading Room had a new role as a mortuary.

During the 1950s, Shanklin as a seaside resort was at its height. Each summer a touring repertory company arrived, putting on two plays a week and tempting visitors to come to the theatre twice. Sunday nights saw grand variety performances. In order to afford celebrities, in conjunction with Sandown Pier, the acts changed venues at half-time, being bussed from one place to the other. In the winter local operatic and dramatic societies filled the stage.

With changing fashions traditional entertainment became less popular. The theatre was hard pushed to attract audiences but thanks to local support, tribute acts, stars of yesteryear, fortune telling and even championship wrestling continue to keep the doors open.

QUARR ABBEY HOUSE

FOR MORE THAN 300 years, the powerful Fleming family owned tracts of land stretching from Binstead to Fishbourne, Havenstreet to Arreton. This included Quarr, named for its stone quarries, where life for the monks at Quarr Abbey had been rudely interrupted at the whim of King Henry VIII. It was here in the 1840s that the Flemings erected a house at Quarr Farm. Constructed mainly from the tumbled ruins of the abbey, it became known, unsurprisingly, as Abbey House.

In 1858, it was leased to an equally substantial family, the Cochranes. The new occupant, Thomas John Cochrane, had followed his family's naval tradition and (aided by his father) was a captain by the age of seventeen. He served in the West Indies, North America and the Far East, and at the end of his career he was Admiral of the Fleet. He died in 1872, leaving his widow Rosetta at Abbey House.

Of their two children, Minna, by virtue of her age (and breeding), became a playmate, lifelong friend and Lady in Waiting to Princess Beatrice, Queen Victoria's youngest daughter. The queen and other members of the Royal family frequently visited and it was to Abbey House that newly married Princess Beatrice and her husband Prince Henry escaped for a brief honeymoon.

MINNA'S BROTHER, TOM COCHRANE, seems to have dedicated more time and money to pleasure. He started naval training but, unlike his father's meteoric rise, by the time he was 25 he was only a Sub-Lieutenant. After his marriage he spent time in Canada, investing in lumbering, cattle and brick-making enterprises, largely driven by his wife, Adela. From 1899 to 1910 he held the post of Deputy Governor of the Isle of Wight, living at Carisbrooke Castle. His post came to an abrupt end when his passion for fast cars and fast living found him briefly in gaol. His misdemeanours were covered up and he was packed off to America.

Rosetta Cochrane, Tom's mother, died at Abbey House in May 1901, being buried with her husband at Kensal Green. The estate was put up for sale in 1907 and the land went full circle.

In the late nineteenth century, a group of French Benedictine monks arrived in England looking for sanctuary. They chose a temporary refuge at Appuldurcombe House at Wroxall. As the lease came up for renewal they looked around for an alternative home, lighting on the empty property at Quarr. Incorporating Abbey House, a new, innovative brick monastery was built, its construction providing work for 300 local men. At the end of the First World War, many of the Order returned to France but a small group remained, leading a monastic life which continues into the present day. Abbey House, as an integral part of the monastery, is closed to the public.

BONCHURCH POND

IT IS DIFFICULT to imagine Bonchurch without its pond. Here wildlife thrives; carp, ducks, moorhens, minnows and herons continually announcing their presence.

The village clings limpet-like to the steep cliffs, peaking at St Boniface Down – a mere 20ft short of being a mountain. Once inaccessible, Bonchurch came late to the notice of visitors, but, having discovered it, they fell quickly under its spell. John Keats was an early disciple while Charles Dickens famously spent a summer at Winterbourne, working on *David Copperfield*. A young Algernon Swinburne lived at East Dene, the only one of Admiral Swinburne's brood not to be born here and the only one to cling tightly to the Island as home. Algernon was fully expected to be either Poet Laureate or win a Nobel Prize for literature, but neither materialised.

The pond itself owes its existence to an 'ovener', Joseph Hadfield. Born in Exeter, Hadfield was coerced into the family firm of silk merchants, growing rich in the process. Interested in the latest technologies, he claims to have launched the first unmanned balloon flight in England and is said to have travelled to America to collect a debt owed to his father of £50,000 plus

interest, in the process meeting George Washington. In about 1800 he moved to Bonchurch, leasing Mackett's Farm. One of Joseph's projects was to clear the marshy osier beds where fishermen once collected reeds to make lobster pots. In its place emerged an ornamental pond. Joseph built a house – Uppermount – now called the Peacock Vane, and erected cannon on a huge rock that came to be known as Hadfield's Look Out to keep watch for Napoleon. Later he moved to Ventnor.

IT IS THANKS to ship's surgeon, doctor and writer Henry de Vere Stacpoole, however, that the pond is as it is today. After a life of roaming the South Seas he married his wife Margaret and settled at Cliff Dene. The pond was included in the estate. His fanciful novel *The Blue Lagoon*, about a boy and girl growing up alone on a tropical island and falling in love, caught the public imagination, spawning films and imitations. In total he wrote about sixty works.

Stacpoole, an avid bird lover, founded The Penguin Club to protect marine birds against oil pollution. When Margaret died, he left Bonchurch Pond to the village in her memory, as a bird sanctuary. Stacpoole married a second time, to Margaret's sister, but he had no children. He died at Shanklin Cottage Hospital and is buried at Bonchurch. Between them, Hadfield and Stacpoole left the Island a precious legacy.

PRINCES GREEN, COWES

COWES IS NOT normally associated with steam engines but in his short residence there, George Robert Stephenson, nephew of the great George who created the *Rocket*, played a significant part in the life of the town.

In 1860, he was elected to the Royal Yacht Squadron. A keen sailor, he took up residence along the seafront in Grantham House and commissioned a yacht from local boat builder Michael Ratsey. He named it *St Lawrence*, commemorating work he had carried out in Canada on the Victoria Bridge over the St Lawrence River.

George Robert was generous to his new neighbourhood. In 1864, he gave the swathe of land in front of his property to the people of Cowes. It was called The Green and was to be used only for pleasure. At the same time he commissioned a cast-iron fountain, to be erected along The Green. Forged in Scotland, this elegant structure with four columns, a central bowl and a fretted, domed canopy exhorted passing walkers to quench their thirsts. It had a makeover in 1987, being painted in striking Wedgwood blue and white. It stands between two later additions of shelters from which to watch the ever-changing sea.

This was not the end to George's generosity. On the marriage of the future Edward VII to the Danish Princess Alexandra, he donated a Portland stone statue of the goddess Flora. She stood on The Green, a few yards from the fountain. Unfortunately, latterly she became a target for vandals and her arm was broken, so she was removed and ended up in storage at Northwood House, once the home of the wealthy Ward family. Like The Green, Northwood House was donated to the people of Cowes. Flora was forgotten until a visiting party of schoolchildren discovered her in a cupboard. The school then raised funds to restore her to her former glory. She was placed in an alcove at Northwood House, where she can be seen today.

ONE CANNOT BE sure how George Robert would have felt but in 1926, Edward, Prince of Wales, the future and uncrowned Edward VIII, also presented a fountain to Cowes. In return, The Green was renamed Prince's Green, by which it is known today.

In 1990 Stephenson's elegant house was demolished and a block of apartments, known as Grantham Court now stands in its place.

THE TOTLAND BAY HOTEL

THE WARD LOCK Guide of 1834 advertised Totland as 'in great favour with those who love a holiday of the restful type'. Here came the rich and retiring, buying up villas, soaking up the sea air – and latterly soaking in the sea.

The development of Totland was an ambitious project overseen by the Totland Bay Estates Company. They bought up land, advertised its delights and rented plots on a 999-year lease. Two local landowners formed the Totland Hotel and Pier Company Ltd, with eighteen shareholders. The London architects decreed that buildings should have a uniformity of style, must be made from bricks, and have red-tiled roofs.

The need for building materials offered a golden opportunity to Henry Dowty, who started a brick works along the Avenue on the corner of what is now Warden Road. He later diversified into chimney pots, finials, ridge tiles and flowerpots, employing as many as fifty men. A Primitive Methodist and founder of Totland's Methodist chapel, he fell foul of local people by permitting his traction engine to work on a Sunday. He also provided the first tarmac-surfaced road in Freshwater. With his own bricks he built himself a house in The Avenue called Lismore that still displays some of the familiar features. Henry died in 1927 at the age of 84.

The first thing to greet day-trippers arriving by steamer was the glorious outline of the Totland Bay Hotel, advertised as 'a fine, noble, brick building with turrets, terraces and sea views'. It also boasted 'the purest spring water'. All started well and pleasure steamers from Southampton, Bournemouth and Portsmouth visited. Round-the-Island trips offered holidaymakers a stunning view of the Island's coastline.

THE DRIVING FORCE and managing director of the Totland Bay Company was Frank Gerard Aman, described as a land agent, who had fingers in projects as diverse as railways, ferries and motor companies. There were plans to extend the railway from Freshwater and make an underwater link to the mainland, but it never materialised. Frank died on the Island in 1936, having donated the War Memorial to the people of Totland.

The Totland Bay Hotel suffered a familiar fate. Occupied by the military during the war then left empty, it deteriorated. By 1972 it did not conform to fire regulations, and, with no alternative plans, it was demolished. In its place stands a block of flats, appropriately named Aman Court.

The pier also suffered, being severed during the war to prevent enemy landing. Resurrected briefly in the 1950s, after a fire it was closed, being later sold to Trinity House for use as a monitoring station. At the time of writing it is undergoing a re-fit. Hopefully it will survive.

HAZARD'S HOUSE AND TERRACE

IN 1611, MR John Speed produced a detailed map of Newport. Today, anyone would recognise where they were for Pyle Street, Crocker Street, Sea Street, Holyrood Street, Quay Street, Lugley Street and the High Street were already named.

At the bottom of the High Street stood Hazard's House, so-called because sceptics confidently expected that it would flood. In 1652, it was acquired by William Stephens, an ambitious 'ovener' embracing local politics. Stephens changed sides during the Civil War, becoming MP for the Island and Recorder for Newport. He was succeeded by his son, also William, who preferred to stay at home and manage his estates. When he died, his advice to his son William III was to avoid public office. Later, the young man regretted not following his father's advice, admitting that, 'I have done ill in disobeying my father's injunction.' Disillusioned and broke, he returned to the mainland.

In 1682, Hazard's House was virtually re-built. The next recorded occupant was Admiral Charles Holmes, taking up residence in the 1720s. Charles was the descendant of the Island's most notorious governor, Sir Robert Holmes, who engineered the defeat of the Dutch navy, finally settling in Yarmouth as Island Governor. Charles ended his days as Governor of Jamaica, where he died in 1761.

In 1806, Sir John Moore, who achieved lasting fame for his heroic defence at Corunna in Spain, spent his final night in England at Hazard's House before setting out for the Peninsula War.

During the early nineteenth century, Hazard's House became a girls' school. Through the female line it passed to the Gubbins family and for a further seventy years remained in their hands until the last Miss Gubbins, Joany, went into a nursing home in 1937.

HAZARD'S HOUSE WAS a rambling building, on varying levels with panelled rooms, a spectacular staircase and a servants' wing. The front faced the High Street, while behind was a substantial garden where Mr George Gubbins, father of the last occupant, erected a terrace of eight dwellings, bequeathing two to each of his children. It was known as Hazard's Terrace.

When the house fell empty, the Isle of Wight Council purchased it. There was an expectation that it was in safe hands but the council had other ideas. Hazard's House stood in the way of progress and in the 1960s it was knocked down to make way for an extension to County Hall. Hazard's Terrace became the council employees' car park.

HIGH STREET, SHANKLIN

SHANKLIN'S CRADLE IS undoubtedly the Old Village. Picture perfect, from here the town spread north along the High Street, extending both inland and towards the cliff. Thanks to the Victorians, almost overnight a frenetic building boom saw the population increase from 355 at the time of the 1851 census to more than 2,000 souls twenty years later. The locals must have wondered what had hit them. In 1862, the splendid post office building opened its doors at the junction of the High Street and Prospect Road. Two years later the first train arrived at the new Shanklin Station. The following year the Shanklin Gas Company held its inaugural meeting, and in 1879 Shanklin boasted a new Literary Institute.

Churches too began to multiply – the new St Paul's in Station Road in 1866, the Church of the Sacred Heart in 1888, and, in 1883, dominating the skyline in the High Street, the newly enlarged Congregational Church. An ambitious project to incorporate both church and school on the same site proved impracticable, so more land was purchased in Palmerston Road to accommodate the school. The new church was designed to hold 357 people in the main body with a further

seventy-two in the gallery. It was faced with local stone and the tower literally towered 75ft into the air, to be topped with a steeple. Public donations brought an added benefit in an illuminated clock. A Shanklin Guide of 1903 remarked that, 'the loud tones of the clock ring over Shanklin at every hour of the twenty-four'.

UNHAPPILY, SHANKILIN WAS bombed in 1945 and the tower suffered serious damage. The tower had to be rebuilt in the 1950s but the spire was not replaced. The clock, perhaps from the shock, remains silent.

Halfway along its length, the High Street forks. At this junction, by 1900 stood the National Provincial Bank of England Ltd, whose manager was F. Colnutt. The bank had been founded in London in 1834 but operated only in the provinces in order that it could issue its own bank notes. The fine building continues to serve its original purpose, having merged with the National Westminster Bank in 1970.

Because of the lie of the land, on the eastern side of the street is a shopping mall. Below the mall, as far as Palmerston Road (where the new school building was erected), a terrace of shops provided everything, from a florist, two butchers, a milliner, baker and grocer, to a gents' outfitter, tobacconist and corn merchant. Just below Palmerston Road, one of the longest surviving Island businesses, John Bailey & Co. Ltd, selling ladies' fashions, has been in operation since 1931.

CHURCH LITTEN

CLUSTERED AROUND THE navigable head of the River Medina, Elizabethan Newport was a low lying, marshy place, its narrow streets broken by three open spaces. At the southern extreme of the town was Cosham Street, later re-named South Street, where the poorest crowded into a jumble of tiny, ill-served cottages. With inadequate sanitation, no effective supply of water and the arrival of boats from the mainland, in 1582 the worst fears were confirmed when plague reached the Island. Newport lost as many as 200 of its people. Even the Island's governor, Sir Edward Horsey, succumbed to the scourge.

Newport being part of the parish of Carisbrooke, it was to there that the dead were taken to be buried, but with the increasing mortality there was no question of carrying the dead to St Mary's Church. A new site was chosen to the south of the town at the archery butts. The ground was consecrated in 1583 and called Church Litten, being the Saxon word for burial ground.

BY 1900 CHURCH LITTEN was full. For nearly fifty years it remained unused, until in 1950 the death knell was finally sounded. The gravestones were dug up and used as paving slabs, the area was landscaped and Newport was presented with a pleasure park. Very few headstones escaped. A lucky survivor was that of John Hamilton Reynolds, a poet who, inspired by his friend John Keats's enthusiasm for the Island, spent his last years in Newport.

One remaining monument still captures the hearts and imagination – to Valentine Gray, a climbing boy, battered to death by his master, his memorial raised by public subscription.

Through the ornate Elizabethan gateway, despite the adjoining road, mature trees shield the park from the traffic. Across the road Marks and Spencer and Morrison's supermarket do brisk trade. Within the park a stunning weeping beech holds pride of place while an elderly yew, long symbolic of cemeteries, may be left over from earlier times.

In the reign of Elizabeth II, twenty-first-century children play here happily, unaware of the heritage below their feet.

THE GARLAND CLUB

WHEN RETURNING WOUNDED from the Peninsular War, Thomas Reynolds Moreton, 4th Baron Ducie, came ashore at Bembridge, allegedly to take the waters. He found the village, then a virtual island, attractively remote and so much to his liking that he bought up land and built a family home called East Cliff. The road on which it stood was named Ducie Avenue.

In 1814, his descendent, Colonel Augustus Moreton, built another house, Hill Grove, possibly designed by John Nash. Father of seven daughters, he also commissioned houses for their future occupation.

Ducie Avenue led directly to the beach and with his neighbour, Captain Ernest du Boulay, Moreton founded the Bembridge Sailing Club. With a brood of daughters and a penchant for entertaining, at the waters' edge he founded The Garland Club, named for the rocks guarding the entrance to the bay. It was intended as a ladies' bathing club. Soon it became the centre of social life in the area.

Bembridge was never a bucket and spade place. Described as a 'seasonal resort for the affluent classes', this was how it liked to be seen. Something of the feel of the place can be gleaned from the account of Lady Augusta Fane, who, in her book *Chit Chat*, rejoiced that 'the little place remains unspoilt and free from trippers, pierrots and other seaside pests!' Instead the moneyed classes played tennis, raced on the water in their russet-sailed Redwing boats and frolicked the night away, dining and dancing at The Garland Club. As Lady Fane reminisced, the elect 'bathe, have cocktails, lunch and tea.' In the evening they 'rocked and twirled' to the rhythm of Clifford Essex's band.

Lady Fane was the sister of Lady Adela Cochrane whose husband, Tom, was Deputy Governor of the Island. On the water, sporty young women with names such as Miss Pinky Fenwick, Miss Dodie du Boulay and Miss Evelyn Moreton competed favourably with the men. Lady Fane commented how poets, painters, actors and statesmen flocked to Bembridge to be drawn into its Shangri-La magic. Among the Garland's members were David Niven and Earl Jellicoe.

USED AS A seaplane base during the First World War, officers from the Royal Flying Corps enhanced the ranks of eligible young men but frolics at the club stopped with the outbreak of the Second World War and the club, thankfully empty, received a direct hit from enemy fire. On the site a fine, modern architect-designed house shaped like a fan was erected, bearing the name of its predecessor. Since 1950, Bembridge has expanded. New bungalow estates have changed its aspect but it still retains an air of finesse, perhaps a wistful longing for its hedonistic past.

THE OLD MALT HOUSE

FROM TIME IMMEMORIAL Newport's prison, or bridewell, stood on a plot of land at the junction of Holyrood and Crocker Street. Here local lawbreakers were incarcerated while serious cases were tried and criminals imprisoned in Winchester – or despatched by the hangman. Between 1814 and 1829, the yearly number of prisoners held in Newport fluctuated between seventy-four and 359. In 1823, a treadmill was introduced for the punishment of 'convicted felons, misdemeanants and vagrants'. It could hold nine persons working in shifts.

The 1830s saw a separate prison for women opening across the road in the old butcher's shop. In 1852, the bridewell became a police station until a purpose-built building opened in Quay Street in 1869. In November 1901, it was announced that the bridewell was to be demolished. There was no shortage of contractors queuing up to knock it down for its place was to be taken by an infinitely more desirable malt house.

THE MALT HOUSE was described as 'an imposing brick structure' with ornamental mouldings, 100ft long by 50ft wide and 60ft high. It was intended to house a new pneumatic process plant for malting the barley. It was the property of brewers Benjamin Mew & Sons.

The heart of Newport has long been connected with brewing. The meeting of the Lukely Brook with the River Medina meant that there was a ready supply of water. Barley was brought in by river and the end product sent out in barrels. At its height, Mew's Brewery was shipping beer to the mainland, China, India and the Mediterranean. In 1850 the business received a boost when it was commissioned to supply ale to Queen Victoria when in residence at Osborne House. The addition of 'by Royal Appointment' now graced their letterheads. To fund its expansion, in 1873 along came Walter Langton, a London timber merchant who was happy to invest £20,000, settling with his wife Letitia at Gatcombe House. At its height, the company owned fifty-three pubs in Newport alone. Special deals were negotiated with the military at Parkhurst, Portsmouth and Aldershot to supply them with ales. The brewery survived the Second World War unscathed but in 1965 it was sold to the Romsey brewers Strong & Co. Three years later, Strong was taken over by the giants Whitbread, who ceased brewing in Newport and used the site as a store. So began the demise of Mew Langton. A serious flood in 1960 followed by a mysterious fire in the malt house (a listed building) meant that permission was granted to clear the site. The clatter of barrels and the clop of horses were replaced by the quiet presence of sheltered housing.

THE ROYAL SPA HOTEL, SHANKLIN

KING CHARLES II's physician, Dr Fraser, first discovered the health-giving properties of a spring emptying through the cliffs at Shanklin. After a brief interest, the waters were forgotten for 200 years until the arrival of Archibald Hinton. Hinton was born in London about 1815 and during his life managed various places of entertainment, such as Anerley Gardens, which offered 'innocent recreation and healthy employment,' plus fireworks.

Hinton attempted something similar in Shanklin. At his seafront property he installed a tank to catch the waters from the cliff, offering them to the public for a small price. He posted the official findings of their efficacy but the uptake was not encouraging. Then, in 1896, the hotel was visited as part of a tour of British spas, after which the Directors declared Shanklin water to be superior to that of both Buxton and Harrogate and compared favourably with the original Belgian Spa town. Hinton installed a pump house, imported fine marble baths for both men and women and the Spa Hotel was born. It stood near to the newly installed lift and opposite the dashing Shanklin Pier. For the pleasure of residents there was a Palm Court, a Winter Garden, a Coffee House, plus free hot or cold fresh water or sea bathing, all within the precincts of the hotel. Hinton proudly advertised the 'first iron

baths in England,' referring not to the tubs themselves but the iron content of the waters. Male and female masseurs were on hand to attend to the bathers. Advertisements asked 'What other Spa could boast, "I am a Marine Spa. I have Mineral Water Baths. I have the sea in front of me also for Baths",' the promoters confidently asserted that one was bound to encounter a celebrated foreigner.

The Royal Coat of Arms decorated the window of the Coffee House following visits from Queen Victoria's daughter, the Empress Frederick of Germany, and her brothers the Dukes of Edinburgh and Connaught. At the outbreak of the First World War, Victoria's son, Prince Heinrich of Prussia, brother of the Kaiser, was in residence and beat a hasty retreat.

THE SECOND WORLD WAR meant a temporary end to activity. The Island was virtually a prison with few people permitted to visit. Worse was to follow. In 1941, a bomb scored a direct hit on the Esplanade. The Spa Hotel was too badly damaged to save but it managed to play a vital role in the war effort. Soon teams of workmen were surreptitiously visiting the site. Inside the shell of the building, a pumping station of monumental proportions was being developed, its purpose to pump oil across the Channel to supply the allies with the vital resource. It became known as PLUTO (Pipeline Under The Ocean). Today, both PLUTO and the Spa Hotel have gone. In their place is a public car park, an anti-climax to the presence of two important Island icons.

THE BARLEY MOW, SHIDE

SHELTERED BY ST GEORGE'S DOWN, Shide, mentioned in the Domesday Book, relied on agriculture and later the presence of the chalk quarry for its existence.

St George's Down was traditionally a site for army musters. On one unhappy occasion, Sampson Saphior, 'a young fellow and pretty shopman', was mortally wounded whiles on exercises. There being no sign of external injury, Sir John Oglander in his memoirs concluded that, 'all the nerves and sinews in the poll of his head were either broken off or with the fire shrunk up.'

In 1875 the first rail link was supplied by the Newport Junction Railway. Its main purpose was to service the chalk pits and a spur ran directly into

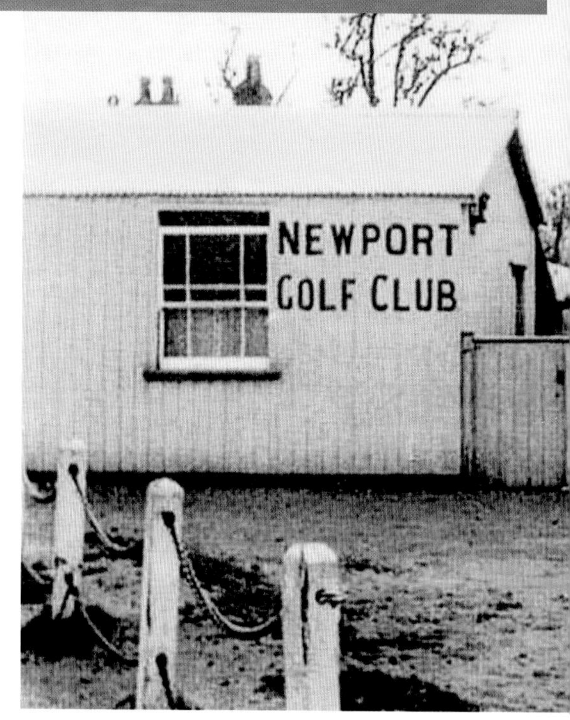

the quarry. Happily for the Barley Mow, the railway station was right next door, while a series of thirsty quarrymen also slaked their thirsts in the bar. The pub was one of many owned by Newport brewers Mew Langton. During the Second World War, production ceased in the quarry and the railway passenger service ceased in 1956. In 1896, Newport opened a Golf Club on St George's Down. The clubhouse was also located conveniently next to the pub, although it has since moved.

In 1851, 36-year-old Daniel Barton was the landlord, although his main occupation was listed as 'wheelwright'. Ten years later he combined the role of innkeeper with brick maker and in 1871 he was still the innkeeper. Clearly the pub trade could not sustain his family, as he was then also employed as a carpenter.

In 1879, Daniel Barton was replaced by William Williams, then, in 1888, by Alfred Lee. By 1900 the pub was in the hands of Mrs Ranger and some time after 1904 it was at least partially rebuilt, with the addition of two gables and a mock Tudor appearance.

REFLECTING THE CHANGING TIMES, in the twenty-first century the Barley Mow has a new name. Recently refurbished it is now a restaurant, known as the Bengal Palace, offering Indian and British food.

THE WHITE HOUSE, PARKHURST PRISON

THE ISLE OF WIGHT is famous both as the former home of Queen Victoria and for an assortment of visiting rogues and murderers. On the eastern edge of Parkhust Forest work began in 1798 on building a permanent barracks. Its doors opened in response to the perceived threat following the French Revolution. Consisting of eight large and twelve smaller barracks, plus five officers' houses, the parade ground was said to be second only to that at Chatham. To the north a hospital provided the best medical care, while in the centre was the surgeon's house, an elegant building painted white with a central clock tower. The buildings on either side have since disappeared and although no longer white, the name survives. A chapel, a laundry and stores provided the necessary services, while a walled garden covering 100 square yards served as a burial ground. The site could house 2,040 men. By 1838, Parkhurst Barracks was ready to close its doors. Britain was suffering a serious case of prison overcrowding, in particular juvenile offenders, who were currently jammed aboard rotting, insanitary prison ships. The solution was to transport them to Australia but meanwhile

they would be housed at Parkhurst for assessment and to learn a trade. On Boxing Day 1838, the first group of 102 boys arrived. Many were employed making and moulding bricks to build two new prison wings. They worked in silence and corporal punishment was routinely administered. *The Times* of 9 September 1843 reported 165 whippings, forty-four confinements in the black hole, and 614 solitary confinements with bread and water.

The youngest child known to be at Parkhurst was 6 years old. As sentence of transportation could not begin until he reached 14, he was held until that time, so his actual incarceration was fifteen years.

IN 1845, QUEEN VICTORIA visited the prison. The boys appeared smart and polite, serenading her with the National Anthem. So moved was she that she granted two pardons.

Things changed in 1863, when 150 female prisoners arrived. If the queen thought that visiting women would be easier, she was in for a shock. The women presented a resentful, brooding presence, turning their backs on Her Majesty and refusing to sing the National Anthem. After her departure things grew worse. Wound up by the visit the women rioted, breaking into the prison yard and tearing off their clothes. Against their wrath the female warders were helpless, calling upon the neighbouring men for help. In view of the seriousness of the situation, it was decreed that only married officers would approach the naked rebels. Armed with blankets and hosepipes, they managed to subdue them.

In 1869, Parkhurst reverted to being a male prison. In 2008, along with Camp Hill and Albany gaols, Parkhurst was amalgamated into HM Prison Isle of Wight.

THE ROYAL SPITHEAD HOTEL, BEMBRIDGE

BEMBRIDGE OWES MUCH of its success to a man described by the *New York Times* as a 'thick, gorged, bloated, monstrosity, rotund, wallowsome and flat footed.' This was Jabez Balfour, founder of the Liberator Building Society, a temperance organisation offering working people the chance to buy their own homes.

Flying high and looking for places to invest the Society's profits, he turned his attention to the Island, embarking on the challenge of erecting a causeway from Brading to Bembridge, draining Brading Haven and opening a rail link from St Helens. Every attempt in the past had failed but in 1878 the work began. By 1879 it was complete and in August a celebratory cricket match was held on the reclaimed land. Within weeks, however, an October storm breached the embankment so that it was back to its original state. Undaunted, a second attempt was undertaken and this time the sea bowed to the success of the project. The cost, financed by the Liberator Building Society, was £420,000.

At Bembridge, Balfour erected a hotel of magnificent proportions guaranteed to satisfy the most discerning visitor. In 1880, having cost £10,000, the Spithead Hotel opened its doors. It was an imposing square building, four storeys high, with dormer windows.

The two prominent wings had bay windows and balconies adorned with intricate fretwork. Driving along the new Embankment Road the hotel greeted the traveller, standing conveniently next to harbour and railway station. Inside it offered a sun lounge, cocktail bar and dancing for its patrons. Outside, one could play croquet and, conveniently, the hotel was also the headquarters of the Royal Isle of Wight Golf Club and a sailing club. The cost of a double bedroom with private bath was 22 guineas per week.

Designed by local architect Samuel Saunders, initially things went so well that an additional storey was added. The Island firm of Ingrams were the builders.

DISQUIET OVER THE funds of the Building Society eventually showed that its assets were grossly over-valued and shortly afterwards it collapsed, taking the life savings of many small investors. Balfour fled the country but was eventually extradited from Argentina and sentenced to fourteen years in prison, serving his sentence at Parkhurst.

The hotel, like many of similar stature, was taken over by the military during the Second World War, from which it never recovered. The pier had gone and in the early 1970s the railway station closed. The hotel was not a listed building and in 1989 it was demolished and replaced by the inevitable block of flats. In 1910, a drinking fountain had been erected outside the entrance to the hotel, dedicated to the Revd James Nelson Palmer and unveiled by Lord Alverstone, then Lord Chief Justice of England. Now, only the fountain remains.

YARMOUTH HARBOUR

NESTLING AROUND THE mouth of the river, one of the shortest routes between the Island and the mainland begins at Yarmouth. The town is one of the oldest Island boroughs, its original charter dating to the twelfth century. Like Newtown, the French attacked it in the fourteenth and sixteenth centuries, but, unlike its neighbour, it recovered and the channel for cross-Solent traffic remained open.

During the reign of Elizabeth I, Yarmouth's population consisted of twenty-six households, but at the same time it sent two representatives to Parliament, a practice continuing until 1832.

The last of King Henry VIII's castles was erected at the mouth of the Yar and a garrison was present for more than 300 years. Often it consisted of no more than six men.

Communication between Yarmouth and the West Wight was impeded by water but in 1706, a ferry service began operating from Yarmouth to Norton, while in 1830 the first

cross-Solent passenger steamship came into the Harbour, later to be taken over by the Railway Company. By 1860 a single lane, wooden bridge spanned the Yar, a toll being charged for its use. The tollhouse stood on the quay on the site of the present Yacht Club. In 1934, the bridge was taken over by the County Council and the tolls abolished. The bridge being too narrow for two-way traffic, traffic lights were introduced, the first on the Island. The lights themselves became a local tourist attraction!

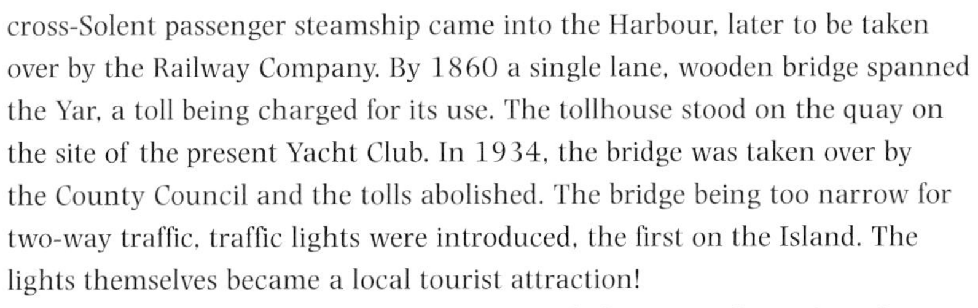

Yarmouth Pier opened on 19 July 1860, and, three years later, the Solent Yacht Club made its headquarters at the George Hotel.

Yarmouth relied on tolls and wharfage for an income. Charges included horses 2*d* each, sheep 6*d* for twenty, coal 2*d* per ton, sporting dogs 2*d*, gunpowder 3*d* per barrel, metals ¼*d* a ton, and potatoes 6*d* a ton. Only fish was exempt.

ACROSS THE RIVER, on the western bank, still stands the Sand House, an eighteenth-century warehouse for the storage of Alum Bay Sand exported to the mainland for glass making.

The old photograph was taken in 1869. It shows the paddle steamer *Emerald* transporting passengers from the mainland, the brig *Rapide*, and a sailing barge. Some time after 1905 the harbour was dredged, while land was reclaimed to build the quay. Old houses were demolished to build new slipways.

The year 1925 saw the first Yarmouth lifeboat, while in 1931, a commission was set up to manage both Yarmouth Harbour and pier.

The town has since grown, and, in the 1980s, the current swing bridge replaced the old wooden structure, while the company Wightlink operates car ferries to Lymington. So far, all attempts to introduce a tunnel have been fiercely resisted.

OSBORNE HOUSE, EAST COWES

AT FIRST GLANCE, the early photograph of Osborne House (taken in 1887, the year of Queen Victoria's Golden Jubilee) looks as if nothing has changed. At the time, however, an important extension was yet to be added – the Durbar Wing.

Newlyweds Victoria and Albert chose East Cowes as the location for their private home, the queen selling Brighton Pavilion to finance the project. In childhood, Victoria had visited nearby Norris Castle and had happy memories of the area.

The Osborne estate was purchased from Isabella Blachford, widow of Robert Pope Blachford, who had made his money through slave trading. Prince Albert designed the new mansion, knocking down the existing house in the process. As the home of the reigning monarch, the ground floor consisted mainly of state apartments, whereas the family's private rooms were on the first floor. The children, of which there were nine, were initially consigned to the second-floor nursery, and a wing was devoted to housing the servants.

On 1 January 1877, Queen Victoria had become Empress of India and thereafter all things Indian were of interest to her. It being considered too dangerous for her to travel to India (in case a revolt at home might occur during her absence),

the sub-continent was brought to her. The queen was taken with the sumptuous decoration at Elvedon Hall, the home of Maharajah Duleep Singh, exiled ruler of the Punjab living in Norfolk. The theme was repeated by her son Arthur in his billiard room at Bagshot Park. It naturally followed that something similar would grace the new Durbar wing at Osborne.

In spite of its size, Osborne had no room of sufficient size to host grand occasions when marquees had to be erected on the lawn.

By 1887, Queen Victoria had spent a quarter of a century as a widow, much of the time shut away at Osborne. Her family had flown the nest and only Beatrice reluctantly remained to act as her mother's secretary. When she rebelled and wished to marry, it took a year to persuade the queen, who agreed only on condition that the couple lived with her. In 1885 the wedding took place. The erection of the Durbar suite allowed for private apartments for Beatrice and Henry.

A TEAM OF twenty-six Indian craftsmen were drafted in to create the Durbar wing, the work supervised by the vice principal of the Mayo School of Art in Lahore, Bhai Ram Singh, overseen in turn by John Lockwood Kipling, father of Rudyard. The decoration consisted of floor to ceiling moulded plaster and papier mâché, richly embellished with Indian images. The centrepiece over the fireplace featured a peacock that alone involved 500 hours of work, while the Elephant God Ganesha offered good fortune. The Durbar wing was completed in 1891. Queen Victoria died ten years later, the house then being handed to the nation by her son, King Edward VII.

THE COUNTY HOSPITAL, RYDE

ON 9 NOVEMBER 1849, the birthday of Albert Edward, Prince of Wales, a new Isle of Wight infirmary opened its doors. It was the first purpose-built hospital for the Island and was the culmination of dedicated fund raising. An initial sum in excess of £6,000 was estimated to be necessary, with a further £600 per year for running costs. A huge boost was added to the project when Queen Victoria agreed to become its patron and the name was changed to the Royal Isle of Wight County Hospital.

The founding father was Mr Ambrose Dodd, a retired physician who had moved to Ryde for the sake of his health. Having volunteered to be secretary to the fund-raising committee, he died in 1847 before the actual building work commenced.

Much of Ryde was in the hands of the wealthy Player and Brigstocke families and it was Miss Player and Miss Brigstock who provided land in upper Ryde, formerly the site of a sandpit. Local man Thomas Hellyer, who was earning a reputation as a church designer, was appointed as architect. The plan was to provide free beds for twenty needy patients plus a further five paying beds. Various ailments were excluded such as tuberculosis, smallpox and venereal disease. The incurables, the pregnant and the insane were also banned, as were children under the age of 7.

In 1855, it was planned to admit casualties from the Crimean War. As money became available the facilities were extended for the treatment of outpatients. A dispensary, kitchen, laundry, nurses' accommodation and an x-ray unit were constructed, and by the time the hospital was complete there was also an eye unit, dental surgery, pathology lab and mortuary.

BY 1892 THE hospital had fifty beds and with the approach of Queen Victoria's Diamond Jubilee it was agreed to construct a children's ward. Fund-raising began with five major donors giving £1,000 each. On 30 August 1897, Princess Beatrice, as Island Governor, laid the foundation stone, and, when the building was complete, Queen Victoria herself officiated at the opening ceremony. Particularly striking was the circular sunroom with its glazed veranda. To further mark the Jubilee a brick and stone arch was erected at the entrance, with a bronze bust of the queen in a niche at the top.

As medical research and new technology progressed, the building became unsuitable for modern treatment and in 1990 it was closed. The hospital was demolished and replaced by modern housing. The queen's arch, complete with a copy of the bust, was removed to the Square in Ryde, while the original bust stands in the entrance to St Mary's Hospital.

WINCHESTER HOUSE, SHANKLIN

WALK ALONG THE cliff top from Shanklin towards Lake, and as you reach the aptly named Skew Bridge, you come to Winchester House. An elegant Victorian dwelling, it was so-named because, in 1893, it was presented to the Winchester Diocesan Council for the use of the Girls' Friendly Society.

The benefactor was Mary Nunn Harvey, whose father had moved to the Island from Nottingham to start a lace-making factory at Newport. Employing the latest technology, he provided work for some 200 people. Mary's only son appears to have died in childhood and she devoted herself to good works.

Mrs Elizabeth Townsend, an Irishwoman, founded the Girls' Friendly Society in 1875 in London. Attached to the Church of England and initially a single-sex enterprise, its hope was that 'the world should be bettered by banded womanhood.' Concerned for the welfare of country girls coming to work in the capital, it provided training, offered friendship, help to the sick, education and books. By the 1920s, it was running summer camps for those who would otherwise not have enjoyed a holiday. Such was its popularity that by 1877 the idea spread to

Ireland, the United States and Australia. In 1884, Queen Victoria agreed to be the patron, donating £50 towards the cause. In 1908, her grandson's wife, Queen Mary, took on the role.

WINCHESTER HOUSE AT Shanklin was easily capable of accommodating up to a hundred young women. For this reason it was probably chosen as the venue for the first World Council, chaired by Mrs Harold Woodward of the USA. Among its founding members were Mrs Harold Browne, wife of the Archbishop of Winchester, and Mrs Jane Nassau Senior, who was Britain's first woman civil servant and inspector of workhouses.

Winchester House was known locally as the Home of Rest, a name still used. During the war it became a convalescent home for the war wounded. When the Society celebrated its eightieth birthday it was again to Shanklin that the delegates flocked. The original building consisted of three wings and faced the sea. Along the seaward length was a veranda with rooms above. The original ethos of training girls to be 'good' moved more towards encouraging everyone to be 'useful'.

Over the years Winchester House has expanded in size and now offers accommodation to both sexes, is licensed for weddings and civil partnerships, hosts various forms of entertainment, themed evenings and caters for parties – a far cry from its original purpose, although the principles remain the same.

THE OLD CHAPEL, THORLEY

THE ISLAND HAS the good fortune to be dotted with tiny villages and some have barely changed in centuries. Apart from one small development, Thorley meanders along the B3401 road to Wellow much as it has always done. Its early growth was due to the navigable reaches of Thorley brook but as the waterway silted up, trading ceased. It remains essentially an agricultural area although the wide grassy plain to the north often becomes a lake in the winter months and is a haven for migrant birds. Bronze Age, Roman and Saxon artefacts confirm that this place has long been occupied. Before the Normans arrived, Thorley was part of the extensive estate of Earl Tostig, brother to the unfortunate King Harold of Hastings fame.

Sometime in the twelfth century, Thorley became a parish and a hundred years later a chapel was built for Amicitia, wife to the Lord of the Isle Baldwin, 6th Earl of Devon. Their daughter, Isabella, was the last independent owner of the Isle of Wight.

The manor house of Baldwin's time has long since disappeared but a footpath will lead you back several hundred years into a secluded burial ground. At its centre stands the porch and bell turret of Amiticia's chapel. This early photograph was taken prior to 1871, for in that year part of the chapel was demolished and a new church erected along the Thorley Road. Both were dedicated to St Swithin.

NEXT TO THE chapel stands Thorley Manor. In the early days of November 1647, King Charles I with his reluctant host Robert Hammond, the Island's governor, was entertained to dinner by John Urry and his wife Jane. Soon after, the king was demoted from the governor's guest to prisoner. The grave of an earlier Urry, John, who died on Christmas Day 1631, remains beneath the old chapel.

In 1869, the Urrys sold the manor to another governor, Sir Robert Holmes, famous as soldier, sailor and explorer. He eschewed the official residence at Carisbrooke Castle, building himself a house attached to Yarmouth Castle. For his only acknowledged child, Mary, he rebuilt the manor house at Thorley. Mary's cousin Henry was induced to marry her with promises of becoming his uncle's heir, a promise he could not resist.

In 1871, the manor was farmed by the Barrington family and in that year the remains of the old church became a mortuary chapel. Numerous tombstones dot the churchyard, most unfortunately illegible. The chapel was granted grade II listed status in 1951.

ST NICHOLAS IN CASTRO, CARISBROOKE CASTLE

IT IS NOT surprising that Carisbrooke Castle, being a Norman fort, also contained a Norman church. King William I, the 'Conqueror', left the Island in the care of his cousin, William Fitz Osbern, and it is he who is credited with building St Nicholas Chapel prior to the Domesday survey. Baldwin de Redvers, the Lord of the Island, then gave the right of appointing a priest at St Nicholas to Quarr Abbey and so it remained until the time of the Dissolution. Thereafter, it returned as the gift of the castle governors.

In 1894, the parish of St Nicholas was absorbed into those at Newport, Northwood and Carisbrooke, but, before that date, the parish included some far-flung lands at Castlehold, Cosham (roughly around South Street in Newport), part of Shide Down, and parts of Rowborough and Dodnor. In its heyday, the chapel served everyone within the parish and what is now Princess Beatrice's garden is believed to have been the castle burial ground.

In 1262, the lord of the castle, Baldwin de Redvers, died and the lordship passed to his sister Isabella de Fortibus, a young widow. He left her extensive holdings in Devon while, through her husband, she inherited vast areas of land in Yorkshire and Cumberland and was probably

the richest woman ever to live on the Island. For thirty years, Isabella lived at Carisbrooke, fighting off all attempts to wrest her power from her through marriage. During this time all six of her children died and when she became mortally ill in 1293, ownership of the castle was taken back by the king.

Isabella preferred to have her private place of worship and in 1269 a new chapel was built inside the castle dedicated to St Peter. The later addition of floors, windows and a staircase now obscure the site. Meanwhile, St Nicholas's chapel slowly decayed. In 1734, the then governor, Lord Lymington, reduced the stonework to within 3ft of the ground and erected in its place a stone and brick building. By 1856, it was again roofless and regarded as a pseudo ruin.

IN 1904, RECOGNISING its history, the chapel was again re-built, the commission going to Percy Stone, the Island's favourite Edwardian architect. It was he who designed the Victoria memorial in St James's Square, Newport. Mindful of Charles I's unhappy stay, the chapel was dedicated to his memory, being consecrated on 30 January the anniversary of his death. A memorial service is still held there each year.

Following the First World War, it was agreed to make St Nicholas the official Island War Memorial, and its walls are panelled with 1,642 names of Islanders who died in conflict.

The chapel has the quaint title of Queen's Peculiar, in that it is responsible directly to the monarch rather than to a bishop.

THE WINTER GARDENS, VENTNOR

PEOPLE ARE WARY of change and plans to demolish the old Ventnor Parsonage in the 1930s met with widespread opposition.

Like most Island coastal resorts, Ventnor mushroomed almost overnight. Prior to 1800 it had a population of about seventy-seven souls, by 1850 that had risen to around 3,000. The heart of the fishing hamlet revolved around two farms and Ventnor Mill. Benefiting from the torrent of water cascading down towards the sea, the mill was recorded as early as 1327. By 1850 it was still hanging on, but in 1870 an accident of tragic proportions occurred when the stepson of the miller fell into the grain silo and was suffocated. By this time the land on which is stood was seen as valuable real estate and sold off for development.

The parsonage, along with the school and St Catherine's Church all owed their existence to the generosity of John Hambrough, who had bought an entire hamlet at nearby Steephill to build himself a castle. The parsonage was situated at the top of the hill leading to the sea, an enviable spot, so when, in 1929, it became available, Ventnor Urban District Council took the opportunity to buy it. Refurbishing it as a public amenity, a competition was held to give the

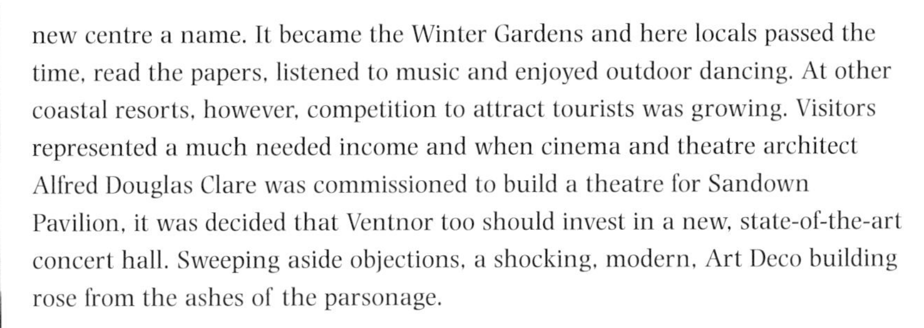

new centre a name. It became the Winter Gardens and here locals passed the time, read the papers, listened to music and enjoyed outdoor dancing. At other coastal resorts, however, competition to attract tourists was growing. Visitors represented a much needed income and when cinema and theatre architect Alfred Douglas Clare was commissioned to build a theatre for Sandown Pavilion, it was decided that Ventnor too should invest in a new, state-of-the-art concert hall. Sweeping aside objections, a shocking, modern, Art Deco building rose from the ashes of the parsonage.

THE NEW WINTER GARDENS easily seated 800 people and could be cleared to allow dancing for up to 1,000. In style it was a miniature version of the de la Warr pavilion at Bexhill, and it opened its doors in August 1936. Whatever the initial outrage and resistance, people soon warmed to its airy space and avant garde appearance. It represented a new era with its fine sprung dance floor, its concerts and talent nights, variety shows and exhibitions.

When Ventnor Council was replaced by South Wight Borough, the Winter Gardens were transferred, and again when South Wight was absorbed into the Isle of Wight Council. The Winter Gardens found it increasingly hard to pay its way and in January 2011, the building was closed. Its future is open to speculation. Whether it becomes a hotel or conference centre, local people regard it as theirs and at the time of writing the struggle to safeguard it continues.

THE FORD, CARISBROOKE

IT IS APPROPRIATE that the modern name of Carisbrooke should incorporate the word brook, for the water flowing through the village is in many ways its lifeblood. Like most other Island rivers and streams, it flows north, rising in the Bowcombe Valley and having to be forded at three places: at the bottom of Clatterford Shute, at Castle Street, and again at the bottom of the High Street.

Right into the twentieth century it powered several corn mills, while the water fed a long-lost eighteenth-century paper mill. The pond to the south of Millers Lane was probably once used for soaking the bark to make paper and the name Paper Mill Field still survives.

The middle of the three fords, at Castle Street, stands cheek by jowl with Carisbrooke Mill. The mill had been established by medieval times and there is evidence of earlier Roman occupation. Its millpond flows behind the Eight Bells pub, now more associated with ducks, swans and boating than with industry. The pond is currently owned by Southern Water, while the mill site is in private hands.

CASTLE STREET CUTS across the High Street from north to south. It is an ancient route starting from the Priory at the top of the High Street, its foundations under the edifice of St Mary's Church. Adjacent to St Mary's was Priory Farm, its pond still extant. From here regular traffic descended, crossing the High Street and fording the stream before climbing again to Carisbrooke Castle. At the Priory there was once a leper hospital.

Two rows of cottages line Castle Street, once workmen's dwellings. The survey of 1861 recorded men working as millers, brewers, bakers, bricklayers, painters, carpenters, wheelwrights, gardeners and errand boys. The wives also worked as charwomen, laundresses and domestic servants. Two of the small cottages each housed nine persons.

Castle Street once offered liquid refreshment. In 1910, the Castle Street Brewery was sold to Mew Langton and it was also possible to take tea at Virginia Cottage.

Halfway down the hill, on the western side, stood the Chapel on the Hill. In 1936, its worshippers moved down the hill and across the road into the Wayfarers Fellowship Hall. The chapel, like the mill, is now a private house.

In truth, Castle Street has changed little. Although no longer a major thoroughfare, it is worth a detour on foot to enjoy its ambience.

EAST COWES CASTLE

IN 1793, 41-year-old John Nash came to the Isle of Wight to visit his friend Admiral Macbride. So far, his life had been something of a rollercoaster. Born in London, he had served his apprenticeship as a monumental mason, worked on the new Bank of England, earned a living as bridge builder in Wales, contracted a disastrous marriage, inherited a fortune and gone bankrupt. Now he was on a high and, liking what he saw, he purchased sixty-nine acres of land at East Cowes intent on building his own residence.

Over the next thirty years, Cowes became his home. Re-married, his wife Mary Anne was the daughter of a coal merchant; she was pretty but regarded by the 'old money' as a vulgar bore. What mattered though was that they were rich and, against the odds, Nash was a close friend of the Prince Regent.

Nash's new house was a fantasy, built around a central tower with views across the Solent. In addition to the main rooms and servants' quarters, he incorporated a billiard room with a domed ceiling and a conservatory. By 1802, the first phase of building was complete. Later he added a library and picture gallery, plus a second conservatory 150ft in length. On wet days Nash is said to have taken his exercise in the conservatory, walking five miles in the dry.

The Prince Regent developed a passion for sailing and on several occasions came to stay with Nash. A new octagonal tower was added to the castle plus a bedroom especially for Prince George, later being known as 'the King's Room'.

In 1815, Nash started work on the Brighton Pavilion, while on the Island he purchased the manor of Ningwood, using the manor house as a hunting lodge. Locally he built the Isle of Wight Institution and the Guildhall in Newport, churches at East Cowes and Bembridge, plus Cowes church tower and Northwood House.

Things began to unravel when the king decided to upgrade Buckingham House. The work fell to a reluctant Nash, then in his seventies. He was accused of financial mismanagement and a public enquiry followed. The scandal denied him the baronetcy he had hoped for. His finances worsened and when he died in 1835 his coffin was removed to the church at dead of night, in case it should be seized against his debts. The castle was sold and Mary Anne moved to Ningwood.

EAST COWES CASTLE then passed through several hands and during the Second World War it was taken over by the War Office. Thereafter it stood empty and thieves stole the lead from the roof. By 1950 it was declared to be beyond repair and all last minute attempts to save it failed. An extensive bungalow estate now leaves little clue as to its existence.

THE LUNATIC ASYLUM, BLACKWATER

JULY 7 1896 saw the grand opening of the Island's Lunatic Asylum. It was the climax of two years' work and much controversy. Until then the insane were shipped to Knowle Hospital, near Fareham. Because of the cost involved it was decided that the Island should have its own facility and money was granted for its construction.

Various sites were put forward but in the end Whitecroft Farm, about a mile distant from Newport, was selected and fifty acres of land leased for the purpose. The contract for the design went to architect B.S. Jacobs of Hull, who had already designed hospitals at Derby and Canterbury. A London building firm won the contract.

The intention was to create a self-sufficient community. For the Island it was a major undertaking, supplying much-needed employment. As a similar development was taking place at Parkhurst, a quarter of the workforce had to be brought in from the mainland.

It was estimated that six million bricks would be needed and they could be made with local clay, but it soon emerged that the output could not keep up with the building programme. More bricks had to be imported, adding to the cost. To speed up their transfer, railway tracks were laid down and horses were kept busy pulling wagons from dawn to dusk. A dispute arose about pay and a strike was called, workers from Whitecroft and Parkhurst rallying in St James's Square. After two days the men returned to work, without their demands being met.

Other problems arose. The water supply was contaminated and two men died of typhoid. A new well was sunk, and safe water stored six storeys up in a tank in the spectacular square water tower, topped by an elegant domed cupola and housing a clock. The main building was joined by an array of kitchens, workshops, laundry, a well house, staff cottages and a lodge.

WHEN THE FIRST patients returned from the mainland, forty men came by train to Blackwater then walked the final mile. The hospital was intended to house about 300 people. Included in the building were facilities for private patients.

Initially, treatment was little more than restraint. Even the paying patients were allowed only one visit a month. Patients worked in the gardens and, through sport, connections were made with the outlying villages, allaying earlier fears.

With the emphasis on 'care in the community', Whitecroft became increasingly irrelevant and in 1992 it closed. For several years very little happened, although the health authority continued to use the laundry and the old nurses' home became offices. Some partial conversion of the main building as housing has taken place, but the future of the entire site is uncertain. Happily, the water tower is now a Grade II listed building.

CHRIST CHURCH SANDOWN – A GARRISON CHURCH

UNTIL 1856, SANDOWN was a part of Brading parish. It may have remained so for even longer had an already substantial church, built to serve the military, not existed.

Sandown Barracks was erected in response to the Napoleonic wars and located at the top of the Broadway. The garrison church, completed in 1845, stands next door. Built in the Early English style, it incorporates a tower and steeple housing a clock and bells. A further aisle was added in 1874.

Taking a royal interest, Princess Victoria, mother of the future Kaiser Wilhelm, donated a window featuring Moses and bearing the Prussian coat of arms. She is commemorated in the Princess Royal Chapel.

Prominent in the church is a memorial to Hugh Edward Richard Boxer DSO, who was last seen commanding the First Battalion Lincolnshire Regiment at Hoogue near Ypres on 21 June 1915. For six months his wife, Jeannie, clung to the belief that he was still alive but in January 1916 the German authorities confirmed that they had found his body. Earlier in his career his foot had been shattered by a Dervish bullet. Jeannie dedicated a plaque and two stained-glass windows to his memory.

In the 1890s, the Duke of Connaught's regiment were serving on the Island and the church also contains a plaque bearing the names of five men who died in South Africa. The First World War memorial includes the name of twenty-six local soldiers.

PERHAPS MOST POIGNANT is the square, stone column in the churchyard dedicated to seven men who died aboard the *Eurydice*, a cadet sailing ship that mysteriously sank off Dunnose Point on 24 March 1878 with the loss of up to 300 lives. There were just two survivors. Between May and October a total of seven bodies washed up at Sandown Bay and were buried in the graveyard, two of whom were never identified.

Christ Church continues as a parish church, while the barracks it once served is now a leisure centre.

THE FIVE BELLS AND THE NEW INN, BRIGHSTONE

THE LANDLORD OF the Five Bells Inn at Brighstone must have been less than pleased when another pub opened its doors right next door, calling itself The New Inn.

The Five Bells advertised 'Beds & Refreshments' and received its deliveries of beer from the Mew Langton Brewery. It took its name from the five bells installed in St Mary's Church tower

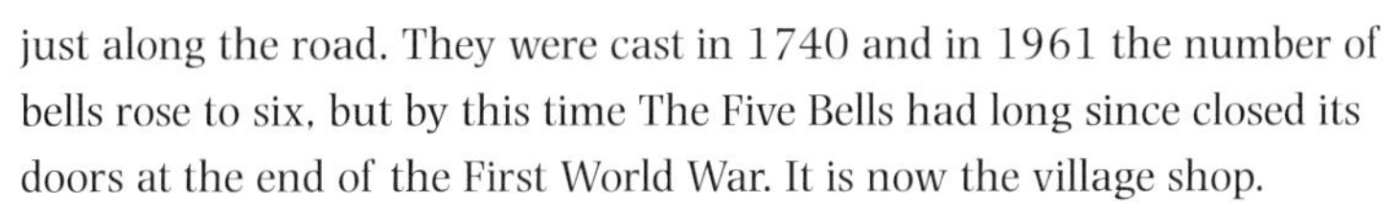

just along the road. They were cast in 1740 and in 1961 the number of bells rose to six, but by this time The Five Bells had long since closed its doors at the end of the First World War. It is now the village shop.

For about thirty years the landlord of the neighbouring New Inn was Job Hawker, a parish councillor and pillar of the community. In 1867, he married local girl Lucy Gillingham and they had one daughter, Edith. Job died in 1923 and Lucy continued as proprietor of the New Inn. She died in 1929. At about this time the pub changed its name to The Three Bishops, commemorating three local rectors who all aspired to a bishopric.

THE EARLIEST BISHOP, Thomas Ken, served for two years at Brighstone before becoming the Bishop of Bath and Wells. Refusing to recognise the accession of King William III, he was imprisoned in the Tower of London and lost his see.

The second future bishop, Samuel Wilberforce, was the son of William Wilberforce of emancipation fame. He is mainly remembered for his condemnation of Darwin's theory on the origin of species and served as Bishop of Oxford. He died following a fall from a horse.

George Moberly served for thirty years as headmaster of Winchester College before retiring to the rectory of Brighstone in 1866. In 1869, he was appointed as Bishop of Salisbury, leaving the Island and thus giving Brighstone its third bishop.

Brighstone remains relatively unspoilt, with many thatched properties and a medieval church dedicated to St Mary. It was the first place in the Island to have an RNLI station, in 1860.

THE DOLPHIN, NEWPORT

AT ANY TIME during the eighteenth/nineteenth centuries one might have found upwards of fifty pubs scattered around Newport. Arriving on a boat at the head of the River Medina, the first one the traveller would have encountered was The Dolphin, standing on the corner of Sea Street and Quay Street. The Dolphin is ancient. The date above the window is inscribed 1758, but this is believed to refer to the time when major repairs took place.

Those earlier sailors and bargemen arrived at a busy port. At the head of the River Medina, warehouses guarded cargoes ready for shipment to the mainland and further. On the western bank the clatter of trucks and the beat of horses' hooves announced the transport of Mew Langton's beers, destined for far-flung places – their India Pale Ale was shipped to India. Coal barges discharged their loads by Coppins Bridge. At the wharf Dunlop and Company traded as corn, coal and lime merchants, while along Sea Street, Dixon and Cardus specialised in artificial manure.

Men waiting for the tide often took refuge in The Dolphin. In December 1813, a fatal duel took place following a chance encounter at the inn. The deceased was Lt Cochrane Sutton, who had planned to leave the following day on the vessel *Grace*, bound for South America.

The *Grace* had been seized by Customs at Cowes for various discrepancies and, because of the delay, the passengers were all kicking their heels. Others awaiting embarkation were Major Orlando Lockyer, Thomas Redesdale and Lt Robert Hand. A casual observation by Sutton that 'we are a parcel of damned idle fellows and are leaving the country to get away from our creditors' upset Lockyer, who immediately accused him of calling him a debtor. As a result the pair, with their seconds, met the following morning at Northwood Park, where Lockyer fired a single shot, hitting Sutton in the heart. The three remaining men promptly vanished but were later arrested and appeared in court at Winchester. In his defence, Lockyear said that even on the way to the duel he had tried to settle the matter amicably, but Sutton would have none of it. The charge was changed from murder to manslaughter and the participants received three-month prison sentences.

APART FROM THE new, imposing brick building incorporating the law courts, Quay Street and Sea Street have changed little. In Quay Street, offices for solicitors, the County Court and the police station rub shoulders with carriers and provision merchants. The street is wide to accommodate trade and the architecture is varied and interesting. The warehouses in Sea Street, where grain and beer were once stored, now house the Quay Arts gallery.

The Dolphin closed its doors in the late 1960s and was converted into flats. It is now a Grade II listed building.

MOA PLACE, FRESHWATER

THE HEART OF Freshwater has a distinctly Kiwi feel. About 1885, Mr George Scorey returned from New Zealand and settled in the village. Whilst abroad he had made money from sheep farming and he returned to invest his capital locally. Acquiring a parcel of land in the centre of Freshwater, incorporating School Green Road and Brookside, he set about building and landscaping it to his satisfaction.

'Old Scorey', as he was known, proceeded to build some cottages, naming them for locations in New Zealand. Thus, Hoki Tika and Opawa (both on South Island) and Wanganui (North Island) grew up on the northern side of the road. Unfortunately, with the exception of Hoki Tika, the names are no longer displayed.

Opposite the cottages was an area of green that Scorey called Moa Place in remembrance of the species of flightless New Zealand bird, now extinct. Scorey's main interest was commercial and the stand of shops on the western side of Moa Green that replaced the old thatched cottages remains today. In the centre, topped by a gable holding a clock, was the shop of James Dimmock, watchmaker.

Curiously, the premises has retained its connection with clocks, being occupied in the 1960s by Awty's the jeweller and in the 2000s by the Clock Shop. A barber's shop has also been a long-term feature and, at the time of writing, each end of the row is occupied by a charity shop (West Wight Cancer Care) and a branch of Boots the chemist.

ALONG SCHOOL GREEN ROAD, to the west of the houses, there was a pub called The Badger. When it burned down, George Scorey used the site to build the biggest hotel in Freshwater in a fine Georgian style of red brick with an imposing façade, called The Standard. Next door he constructed the equally prestigious Assembly Rooms, making a focal point for lectures and meetings. In 1900, George was the proprietor of the Assembly Rooms, living in Standard Cottage, while Walter, his son, was the landlord of the Royal Standard Hotel. Quite how it acquired the epithet 'Royal' is uncertain.

Sadly, the Assembly Rooms burnt down in 1929. Hurst's the hardware store, the Hong Kong Express and the Red Cross shop now occupy the space. The Standard continued to trade for nearly a hundred years but now stands empty awaiting its fate. Perhaps George Scorey should be commemorated in some small corner of his empire?

BARRINGTON ROW, CALBOURNE

FEW ISLAND VILLAGES remain as unspoilt as Calbourne. Traditionally it was the epitome of rural life, its cottages providing labour for the ancient Swainston and Westover estates, its parishioners worshipping at All Saints' parish church, the children attending Calbourne School and the men drinking in The Sun Inn. All too briefly the railway passed through and the road was re-routed, placing The Sun Inn on the opposite side, but otherwise things remained much the same.

The lifeblood of the village was the Caul Bourne, a busy stream flowing from Westover Down north towards the sea at Yarmouth. On its way it powered five mills, providing work and income for local families.

At the turn of the nineteenth/twentieth century, the row of tiny agricultural labourers' cottages along the Caul Bourne at Barrington Row became the focus of an already dying way of life, somewhere to be visited and indulge in a spot of nostalgia.

BARRINGTON ROW HAS two names. The Barringtons were a wealthy family living at Swainston Manor. The manor itself started life as a palace serving the bishops of Winchester and its thirteenth-century chapel remains. In the early nineteenth

century, a family marriage with the Simeon family changed the name but the lane in front of the Caul Bourne remained as Barrington Row.

Its alternative name is the quirky Winkle Street. Among suggestions as to its origin is that 'winkle' is an ancient name denoting a lane that goes nowhere; that it takes its name from John Winkle, fourteenth-century rector of Shalfleet; or simply that the shells from winkles collected from Newtown Creek were deposited alongside the stream.

Now rather quaint, Winkle Street was once an overcrowded, insanitary place. In 1891, a typical dwelling was No. 1, occupied by Frank and Mary Pitman and their three children, plus a lodger. Frank was an agricultural labourer born, like his children, in Calbourne. Mary had migrated from Shalfleet while the lodger, Edmind Whithington, a 51-year-old general labourer, was also a Calbourne man. Almost without exception the rest of the row was occupied by Calbourne natives with the occasional 'foreigner' from Thorley or Brook.

Sheep played a vital role in village life and the sheep wash along the Caul Bourne continued to be used until 1976. At the time of writing the cottages are much sought after – as long as you don't mind tourists peering through your windows.

THE HERMIT OF CHALE

IN TIMES PAST, it was up to the local community to look after the disabled. This was the case with Isaac Sheath, born in Chale village in 1835. There can be little doubt that he was less than able because the census of 1891 recorded him as an 'imbecile since birth', while in 1901 he was marked down as being 'feeble minded'. This did not stop him from being a memorable resident and owning his own home.

Isaac's parents, William and Jane, had an assortment of children. In 1841 they were living at Stroud Farm in Chale, where William worked as an agricultural labourer. As often happened, at each hiring they may have found themselves with a different master living on a different farm and so it continued until 1881, by which time William and Jane had both died. Isaac then branched out on his own and found lodgings with the Creeth family, who took in

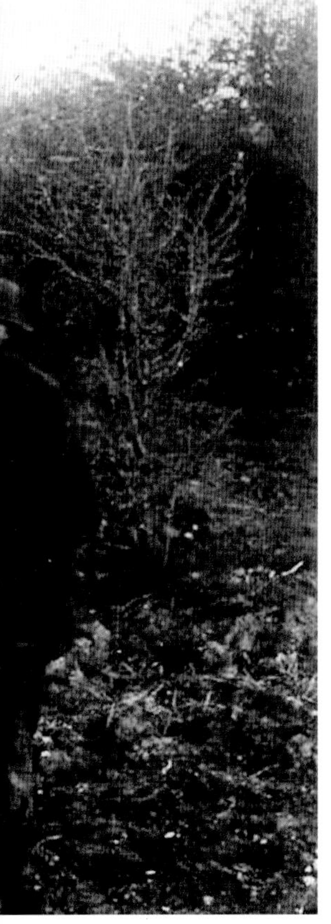

boarders to make ends meet. How long he stayed is uncertain but by 1891 he was listed as 'living at Northgrounds Cottage' and working as an agricultural labourer.

Isaac's 'cottage' was not the stone, thatched dwelling that immediately springs to mind. In fact it was a wooden hovel dug into a bank along Appleford Road. Here, with the help of local people, he managed to scrape a living, receiving hand-outs of coal and items of furniture – although Isaac allegedly found a better use for them as firewood.

APART FROM ANY casual work he could find, Isaac took an early advantage of the tourist season. As the word spread, coach parties made a detour to gawp at his ramshackle home. Isaac obliged by posing for photos, in return for which he expected payment.

If Isaac was popular with visitors, local children made his life a misery, calling him names and throwing stones down his chimney. By 1910, it was agreed that his house was unfit for habitation and he was carted off to the workhouse. Although he was assured of a bed and a meal, he still pined for Chale and freedom. He died in 1912 and the *Isle of Wight County Press* printed an obituary. In his own way Isaac left his mark on the village. Nothing remains of his house but passing by Northgrounds Farm, one might raise a metaphorical hat to the Hermit of Chale.

THE GRANITE FORT, SANDOWN

EXPECTING TROUBLE FROM a volatile Europe, Lord Palmerston commissioned a series of forts to be built along the Island's coast. Particular attention was paid to Sandown, where enemy shipping could easily take advantage of the bay and would not be inhibited by towering cliffs. To this end, work on Sandown Fort commenced in 1861.

This would be the third fort to be built in the area. Henry VIII's Sandown Castle lasted for about a hundred years, before being threatened by the tide. A little further inland, Sandham Fort made an appearance just before the English Civil War, but after 200 years it was outdated and a

third fortification was planned in its place. The replacement of the existing fort caused an unforeseen tragedy. With just nine months to serve before his pension, Sergeant William Whitworth requested permission to stay on but was refused. On 18 May 1760, while his wife slept, he cut her throat and those of his six children. He was charged with their murder but, being found insane, was assigned to a lunatic asylum.

As its name implies, the Granite Fort at Sandown was constructed on the seaward side of huge blocks of granite weighing up to six tons each and hauled from Brading Harbour by teams of horses. The less vulnerable walls to the west were mainly of brick. Special iron plating was added to give maximum protection. During construction the specifications were frequently changed and it was not until 1876 that it was finally fully armed and manned. In the meantime, it had proved a useful training ground for the Isle of Wight Militia.

THROUGHOUT THIS TIME, progress in developing artillery had been swift and the fort was quickly outdated. Ironically, it had been so well built that it proved impossible to adapt its existing layout and update it.

In 1930, the fort was sold for scrap but the new owners confronted the same problem, being unable to dismantle the granite walls. During the Second World War, it housed a machine-gun emplacement and was then identified as an ideal place for a pumping station to transport vital oil to Europe. The project known as PLUTO pumped hundreds of gallons of oil beneath the ocean daily.

After the war, Sandown Town Council acquired the fort and opened the Island's first zoo. Later, it was purchased privately and specialises in the conservation of big cats, in particular tigers.

LAKE HIGH STREET

LAKE IS ONE of the six wonders of the Isle of Wight. In the absence of a body of water, the mostly likely explanation for the name is that it refers to William Atta Laca, who farmed Black Pan in the thirteenth century. The stream that originally supplied water is now underground.

The main thoroughfare between Shanklin and Sandown passes along Lake High Street beginning at Skew Bridge and ending at the top of Lake Hill. In the nineteenth century the manor of Lake was in the hands of Edward Granville Ward, a member of the powerful family that owned lands from Cowes to Totland. The original manor was replaced by the present building, a public house, dating from the early 1900s.

Between the Stag Inn and the old manor house is Lake's shopping centre. The Stag Inn dates from about 1840 and was graced with a carving of a stag above the entrance, now sadly absent. For two decades the landlord was Simeon Trinder.

Just along the road worked Frank Snudden, a carpenter. The Snuddens ran an upholsterers and undertakers business, now taken over by funeral directors Downer and White.

On the corner of Sandown and Newport Roads stood the toll cottage, one of fifty across the Island until the tolls were removed in 1889. The cottage later became the post office.

The year 1891 saw the arrival of the Working Men's Club, followed a year later by the Church of the Good Shepherd, designed by architect Temple Lushington Moore. A Methodist chapel pre-dated it, built just to the north. The original Methodist chapel dated from about 1877 and has in turn been replaced by a mid-twentieth-century building.

IN THE MID-TWENTIETH CENTURY, the premises of the Isle of Wight Co-op gave way to the Screen de Luxe cinema, since closed. New businesses like the Chinese takeaway and the Kebab House reflect the changing times, while a combined post office and general store now stands on the opposite side of the road.

Looking towards Shanklin and prominent on the skyline once stood the chimney belonging to the electricity station based just beside Skew Bridge. When it closed, Farmers' Dairies Ice Cream factory obtained the site, offering waxed paper tubs of rather more ice than cream. That in turn closed and the site now houses an inevitable block of flats.

In 1987, Lake finally got a railway station. The sense of a country village has gone but in general Lake remains the same; less ambitious than its two neighbours but quietly thriving.

ST JAMES'S SQUARE, NEWPORT

ARRIVING BY BOAT at Newport, medieval travellers found a thriving economy. First they came to the Audit House for the transaction of the town's business (roughly where the Guildhall stands), then to St Thomas's Square. With its already old church and market house, the Square had as neighbour the fish and flesh shambles. Finally they reached St James's Square, where much of the town's commerce was conducted.

Newport was granted the right to hold a market as early as 1184. From 1582, the beast market was held regularly in St James's Square and within living memory Tuesday was still referred to as market day. A market also took place on every Saturday and every alternate Wednesday, trading in corn, malt, flour and timber.

The Square has always been filled with activity. Allegedly, in Tudor times, a woman was burnt at the stake for witchcraft. There was once an annual Whitsun fair while for three 'Bargain' Saturdays around Michaelmas, hiring fairs took place.

A hundred years ago, thirsty traders were spoilt for choice, having The Bell, The Red Lion, The Hare and Hounds, The Lamb and The George within the Square. Only The George remains.

In 1890, The Hare and Hounds was knocked down, to be replaced by the Corn Exchange, which in turn was swallowed up by Barclays Bank. Of The Lamb at the other end of the row, only the tiles remain outside the Woolwich Building Society.

On the opposite corner still stands the Isle of Wight County Club, designed by John Nash in 1810. Earlier, the land had been leased to install a cistern, providing river water, one of many abortive plans for the town.

A FOUNTAIN AND drinking trough stood where the Square and the High Street meet. Some time after 1901 it was demolished to make way for Percy Stone's monument to Queen Victoria. It was joined in 1982 by a bust of Earl Mountbatten, the Island's governor, who was killed in Ireland. The solid stone plinth dwarfs the bronze bust it supports.

A second drinking fountain in red marble graced the Square, standing close to the junction with Pyle Street, one of several donated by Sir Barrington Simeon of Swainston Manor. It now moulders on Newport Quay.

Over the decades the market square also served as the bus station, until congestion was such that after 350 years the cattle were moved to South Street. In changing times the cattle market ceased, the site currently occupied by Morrisons supermarket. The bus station also moved to South Street, recently refurbished and fronted with clothes shops.

The market tradition continues, with a farmers' market held on Fridays.

NEWPORT POWER STATION

AS EARLY AS 1813, gas was replacing oil for street lighting. In Newport, work began on Newport Gas Works in 1851 and it was nearly fifty years before electricity presented a serious threat to its dominance.

The superior brilliance of electric lighting had been demonstrated in Newport by the presence of Baker's travelling fair over-wintering at the Drill Hall. With the use of a traction engine, Mr Baker illuminated the neighbourhood and by 1901 the Electric Light Company had a contract to install test cables around Newport Quay, reaching as far as St James' Square and Carisbrooke Road.

The Gas Company didn't give up, pointing out that they were cheaper and that the new lighting did not give off welcome heat, as did the old gas mantles. Members of Newport Council

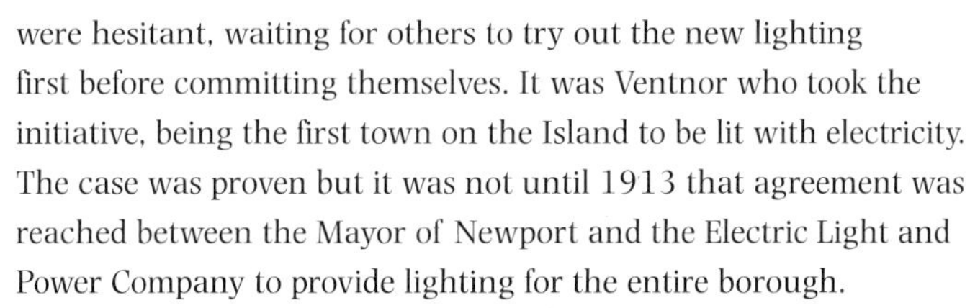

were hesitant, waiting for others to try out the new lighting first before committing themselves. It was Ventnor who took the initiative, being the first town on the Island to be lit with electricity. The case was proven but it was not until 1913 that agreement was reached between the Mayor of Newport and the Electric Light and Power Company to provide lighting for the entire borough.

THE SITE CHOSEN for the new turbine hall was on the western side of the River Medina, just north of the quay and rising up behind The Bargeman's Rest pub. The whole was to include two industrial size sheds, one to house a boiler room where coal was fired and the second to accommodate the turbines, plus a series of other offices and control centres. For the main part, however, the public would have been aware mainly of the frontage, its magnificent stepped gables in yellow brick, faced with red.

The building opened at the start of the twentieth century but with advances in technology, it was operational only until 1927, since which time it has largely been redundant.

At the time of writing its future is undecided. Because of its iconic façade, the council seem inclined to preserve it while disposing of the industrial history it houses. Most of the contents have gone but a movable crane, running the length of the turbine hall, remains, used to lift the machinery out for maintenance. Meanwhile, the battle for its future continues.

COOK'S CASTLE, WROXALL

THERE WAS A time when walkers crossing St Martin's Down could stop to take tea at Cook's Castle. Perched in the lee of the Down, the building certainly looked like a fortress surrounded by stone walls and sporting a high hexagonal tower. You could be forgiven for expecting to come face-to-face with a garrison, but there the resemblance ended. According to the Historic Environment Action Plan (HEAP), in 1774 Sir Richard Worsley of Appuldurcombe House erected a now crumbled obelisk to his ancestor, Sir Robert, and 'at about the same time he also erected Cook's Castle, a folly nearly two kilometres to the East of Appuldurcombe Park.'

Whether it was ever lived in is open to question. At one time it was a substantial building and in summer people were present who, for a charge, would allow visitors to ascend the tower to enjoy the view – and what a view. From the top there was a panoramic sweep to the west, and

turning the tables, Appuldurcombe House, the Freemantle Gate and the Worsley Monument all provided interesting landmarks to ponder. Follow the eye to the east and fields and woodland eventually gave way to Shanklin, Sandown and the white cliffs of Culver. Having admired the landscape, afternoon tea and hot water could be provided on request. Adding to the authentic feel, two cannon guarded the gateway, said to have come from the Earl of Yarborough's yacht, the *Kestrel*. The earl inherited the Appuldurcombe Estate through his wife, and was instrumental in founding the Royal Yacht Squadron. Pelham died appropriately at sea in 1846.

By the time George Brannon produced an engraving of Cook's Castle in the 1840s it was described as 'an ancient ruin', while *Black's Guide to the South East of England* in 1861 referred to it as 'a mimic ruin which overlooks an extensive prospect.' At the turn of the last century there was still plenty of it left, as evinced by contemporary photographs, but by 1913, in her 'wanderings' around the Island, Ethel C. Hargrove observed that it was 'now a shapeless ruin'.

COOK'S CASTLE SEEMS to have declined of its own volition, gradually crumbling away. On 18 August 1940, a plane crashed near the spot. Perhaps the impact shook the already fragile remains, hastening their demise. The stone was probably carted away for use elsewhere.

Today, it is worth visiting the spot where once the castle surveyed the world. One can still follow the route behind St Blasius Church at Shanklin, or take the V30 footpath from Wroxall, skirting the deep side of the Down. Trees obscure much of the panorama but there are still some breath-taking views. On a plateau, sheltered from the prevailing wind, a stone cairn nestles amid the nettles carved with the legend 'Site of Cook's Castle'. This alone bears witness to the existence of this once eccentric icon.

DIAMOND JUBILEE MEMORIAL, WROXALL

WEDNESDAY, 27 APRIL 1898 saw the culmination of village plans to erect a fitting memorial to mark Queen Victoria's Diamond Jubilee. After deliberation it was agreed to install a brick and stone drinking fountain, incorporating a clock, a stone plaque and topped by a street lamp. The site chosen was at the bridge in the centre of the village. In the same year, the Wroxall Water Works was opened.

After a flurry of similar ceremonies across the Island, there was no royal presence to mark the occasion, although Mr Charles Pittis of the Isle of Wight Council was in attendance. The task of organising the day fell to the head of the committee, Mr John James Francis, headmaster of the mixed infants' school, while the honour of placing the commemorative plaque fell to Mrs White, wife of the vicar.

The street was decorated with bunting while a large Union Jack – and rather more surprisingly the Star Spangled Banner – franked the monument. Mr William Flux of Cleveland Villa made the opening speech. He explained that thanks to generous private donations, the committee had raised the majority of the money required but that there was still an amount outstanding and he called on local residents to make up the shortfall. He also praised the ladies of the fund-raising committee for their sterling work.

Mrs White then mounted a specially prepared platform and as the crowd waited, she applied a bed of mortar to the base, after which the contractor Mr John Wallis, a local mason of Clarence Road, lowered the stone into place. To round off the occasion, Mrs White was presented with a bouquet of flowers and all present sang the National Anthem.

THE FOUNTAIN WAS a focal point of the village but with time it faded into the background, largely unnoticed until, in 1970, residents awoke to discover that it was gone. Plans were afoot to widen the road and without any local consultation, it was simply removed and its fate is unknown. Local people objected to the high-handed action and only after considerable pressure did the council grudgingly add a plaque to the remaining bridge with the original dedication: DIAMOND JUBILEE MEMORIAL 1837 – 1897.

THE RAILWAY STATION, SANDOWN

23 AUGUST 1864 saw the residents of Sandown turning out to witness an historic occasion. The first passenger train from Ryde to Shanklin arrived at Sandown Station.

Considerable care had gone into the design of the building, a two-storey construction to include not only a booking hall and ticket office, but also accommodation for the stationmaster. The whole was constructed in yellow brick topped with a gabled, pitched roof. The owners were the Isle of Wight Railway Company.

Initially with just one platform, by 1868 a second line was planned from Sandown to take goods and passengers from Sandown to Newport then on to Cowes. This project was under the auspices of the Isle of Wight Central Railway and Sandown was now a junction station. This additional line opened in 1875 and Sandown became the headquarters of the Isle of Wight Railway.

Clearly the extra traffic called for an extension of the facilities. A second platform was erected with a double canopy 200ft long with an ornamental wooden frieze, keeping passengers dry on whichever side of the line they were waiting. Because of the

layout, there was little room in the vicinity and the signal box was placed high on the roof above the two platforms. New sidings came into use and a subway linked the platforms. To the west were the coal yards and goods yards.

Meanwhile, further additions enhanced the railway buildings. At the south end an ornate single-storey extension resembling a church and complete with tower, incorporated a refreshment room. WH Smith provided passengers with reading matter, a station clock ensured punctuality, while Fry's chocolate could be obtained from a slot machine. Across the concourse the Terminus Hotel offered suitable lodgings.

Soon there was insufficient room for the stationmaster so a house was rented across in Nunwell Street where, in the adjoining fields, horses and carriages were available to carry the gentry onwards to their destination.

IN 1923 THE Island routes were amalgamated into Southern Railway. Sandown continued to see plenty of traffic but in the drastic cuts of the 1960s the Island's lines were deduced to the single route from Ryde to Shanklin. Gone are the refreshment rooms, the signal box and the coal yards but happily the station survives.

If you enjoyed this book, you may also be interested in …

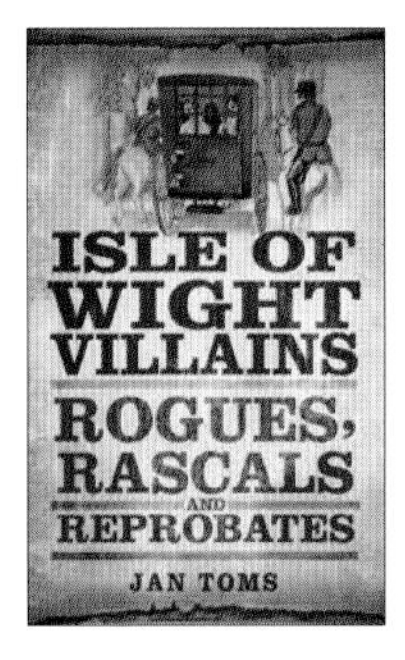

Isle of Wight Villains: Rogues, Rascals and Reprobates

JAN TOMS

Once renowned as a place to dump criminals, and with a past steeped in smuggling, the Isle of Wight provides copious tales of corruption, violence and delinquency. Featuring criminals such as Michael Morey, who butchered his grandson, and thirteen-year-old John Leigh, who strangled his father and, caught in the act by his sister, threw her from a window, *Isle of Wight Villains* details the darker side of this island paradise.

978 0 7524 6219 6

The Little Book of the Isle of Wight

JAN TOMS

Did you know? A new species of cat-like dinosaur, yet to be named, was discovered on the Isle of Wight in 1988. Darwin began his world-famous *On the Origin of Species* while staying at the Kings Head Hotel. There are 21 tourists to every Island resident. *The Little Book of the Isle of Wight* is a fact-packed compendium of the sort of frivolous, fantastic or simply strange information which no one will want to be without.

978 0 7524 5817 5

Hampshire and Isle of Wight Folk Tales

MICHAEL O'LEARY

These beautifully told folk tales, featuring dark tales of murderous kings and commoners, wild women, screaming skulls, galloping plague coaches, dragons dancing themselves to death, giants, and wandering corpses, combined with humorous stories and evocative tales of love, lust and passion, takes the reader beyond the written page and reveals the wonders that lie within the Hampshire landscape.

978 0 7524 6123 6

The Accidental Assassin

JAN TOMS

When Victor Green receives a letter from the council telling him to prune a lime tree in his front garden, he is anxious to oblige. But when a disgruntled pigeon startles him and he falls from the tree, he lands on a passer by – a gangster generally known as Gruesome – and Victor's life is turned upside down. Making friends and enemies along the way, as well as leaving a trail of bodies in his wake, Victor's adventure will leave you laughing out loud.

978 0 7524 6270 7

Visit our website and discover thousands of other History Press books.

www.thehistorypress.co.uk